BRISTOL CREAM

1 A commemorative painting by Captain Weekes showing the *Bristol*, 459 tons (right), and the *Aeolus*, 278 tons (left). Captain Thomas Harvey, senior, was master of the *Bristol* from 1807 to 1819, and Captain Thomas Harvey, junior, was master of the *Aeolus* from 1809 to 1811 and from 1813 to 1818

BRISTOL CREAM

Godfrey Harrison

London
B. T. BATSFORD LTD.

First published 1955

Printed and bound in Great Britain by Jarrold and Sons Ltd.
London and Norwich, for the Publishers
B. T. BATSFORD LTD.
4 Fitzhardinge Street, Portman Square, London, W.1

PREFACE

"BRISTOL CREAM" is the name of a famous sherry. It is the property of Messrs. John Harvey & Sons Limited, of Bristol. This book too is theirs. It would not have been begun, and could not have been finished, but for them and particularly their chairman, Mr. John St. Clair Harvey. It is the story of the Harvey family's connexion with the wine trade in Bristol during some 130 years, and of the firm whose history goes back further still.

Many priceless old records went up in flames, along with Harvey's ancient headquarters, in an air raid in 1940. It has been my task to gather and reconstruct as much as possible. In this I received unstinted help from them. The memories of senior members of the staff and the family, with whom I have spoken at length, threw a clear light on some aspects of the trade and of Bristol society as far back as the closing years of the nineteenth century; I only wish I could set down their recollections as vividly as they were imparted to me.

The present directors' knowledge of their trade is, it goes without saying, profound. Of this I have tried to convey a little—for the mysteries of wine are fascinating—while avoiding technicalities which might interest only the fortunate few.

The story of a family business cannot be detached from its background; it focuses on an individual point the events of a wider sphere and a longer stretch of time. The background of this story consists of the port of Bristol and its age-old connexion with wine; a subject which has drawn me on, intrigued by its incidents, its character, and its consistency in many points from century to century. It has led me further both in space and time than I ever expected. Yet all seemed relevant. Many details collected from far away and long ago were parts of one large, colourful tapestry against which the action of the play must inevitably take place.

There are books about Bristol and books about the wine trade, written by those who have known them longer and studied them more deeply than I. I have drawn upon many of them; and I must mention particularly *A History of the Wine Trade in England* and other works by M. André L. Simon; Latimer's *Annals of Bristol*; W. Hunt's *Bristol*; Professor MacInnes's more recent book, *A Gateway of Empire*; and the writings of Miss E. M. Carus Wilson. For the rest I must thank Mrs. Patrick McGrath, who supplied me with a good deal of material; Miss Elizabeth Ralph, City Archivist of Bristol; Mr. F. G. Webb of the Port of Bristol Authority; and Mr. R. C. Jarvis, Librarian to Her Majesty's Customs & Excise, King's Beam House, London, and his staff. Mr. Bryan Little, historian of Bristol, kindly read the proofs and made a number of useful suggestions; the Appendix, "Some Harvey Wine Lists" was contributed by Mr. Edmund Penning-Rowsell.

I have had much good advice and expert guidance—more you may think, than the modest results justify. I wanted to be able to say that I had written nothing but fact. That would be a bold claim, for the facts are not always certainly known, and generalizations sometimes require endless qualification.

What I can say is that pains have been taken to get as near as possible to the truth, and that no detail has been used which did not seem, on the evidence, at least probable. There are two exceptions—incidents where imagination has been allowed to take a hand. These come at the beginning and at the end, and are easily recognized for what they are.

Summer, 1955   GODFREY HARRISON

CONTENTS

ACKNOWLEDGMENT

THE Author and the Publishers wish to record their grateful thanks to the following for supplying illustrations and for granting permission for them to be reproduced in this book.

The dust-jacket design and figures 2, 10 and 19 are reproduced by courtesy of the City Museum and Art Gallery Committee, Bristol.

Figure 33 is reproduced by courtesy of the Port of Bristol Authority.

Figures 7 and 17 were supplied by *Picture Post* Library.

Figure 8 is reproduced from a photograph by M. Gueugnon of Dijon.

The remainder of the illustrations have been taken from the collections of John Harvey & Sons Ltd., and the Publishers.

LIST OF ILLUSTRATIONS

The numerals in parentheses in the text refer to the figure numbers of illustrations.

The illustrations in the text are taken from Wine, the Vine and the Cellar *by Thomas George Shaw, 1864. The decorations on the half-title pages are reproduced from a design by Reynolds Stone for Harvey's French wine label.*

INTRODUCTION

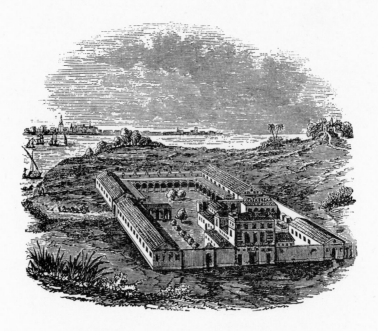

RESIDENCE AND *BODEGA* AT PORT ST. MARY

In the Year 1796

THE house stood in Denmark Street, in the shadow of St. Mark's Church. Its front was solid and dignified rather than beautiful. The stone doorway and heavy door of nail-studded oak were clearly of an earlier period than the rest. The cellars beneath were very much older still: their stout pillars and buttresses were said to have belonged to the monastery of St. Augustine when the abbot's orchards sloped down on either hand to the river Frome.

It was of the cellars that William Perry was thinking as he locked the great door and dropped the key for the first time into his pocket. Soon the dark, cool spaces of the vaults would be filled with sleeping casks of wine. This was to be both his home and his business headquarters.

He turned and walked down the street to its lower end. The river before him was crowded with ships and lined with warehouses. Mingled with shouts and sailors' songs he heard the ring of hoofs and rumble of iron runners on smooth-worn cobbles; for the ground beneath was honeycombed with cellars like his own, full of rich merchandise, for whose greater safety no wheeled traffic had been allowed here in times gone; and even now some of the old sleds remained in use.

Away to his right the Frome joined another river, the Avon; and the Avon went on to join the estuary of the Severn—the Bristol Channel; and from thence the lines of shipping radiated north, south, east and west, but especially west. This was Bristol, a city whose greatness rested on trade, a city whose trade had been shaped by geography.

Its wealth was founded on the varied products of all the world, but in the past chiefly on two: wool, grown, spun and woven in this part of England; and wine, a product of sunnier lands, but one on whose development English

15

merchants had had a decisive influence, and Bristol merchants more than those of any English town but London.

To Perry's left, beyond the river, the old original town stood on its mound, its skyline broken by the towers and spires of countless churches. More churches dotted the hill at his back; and before him, away beyond the two rivers and the low-lying land between, was St. Mary Redcliff, the noblest parish church in England. These and other glorious buildings were the legacies of citizens who had become rich in trade. Here was evidence of a human spirit, and a highly individual spirit, at work. For Bristol was a city shaped not only by the impersonal workings of geography and economics but also by the character of its sons.

Above the oily-looking tidal water and the smells and racket of the quay, criss-crossed by the masts and rigging of a tall West Indiaman, the hills of Somerset hung blue and ethereal. This was Bristol, a city of contrasts. Beauty rubbed shoulders with squalor here, sleepy complacency alternating with vital energy as the soft air of the west with the boisterous tang of the sea. The merchant adventurers of Bristol had sailed abroad for centuries in search of gain; and they had been successful. They were men of commerce, avoiding war when they could; but they fought like tigers when called on to defend their trade. They enjoyed the good things of life with a remarkable zest; was not Bristol Milk a name for fine sherry everywhere? Yet they had built these churches in simple piety. This was no paradox for them. All their ambitions for this world and the next were focused in the city of their birth.

William Perry was thinking of the present as he stood alone on the quay. He was estimating his chances of success. Until this accursed war Bristol had been flourishing. The West Indies trade in particular had been going from strength to strength. Two-thirds of all the ships he could see had brought sugar from the plantations to feed Bristol refineries, and rum and molasses, cotton, tobacco, and strange woods to make dyes for West of England cloth. They would return laden with goods for the plantations—bricks, tiles, hardware, cutlery, cloth, boots, small-shot, nails, all manufactured in Bristol and the neighbouring towns as far as the west Midlands—and sherry and port from Bristol cellars.

This was a grand trade: but even before the war there had been signs that all was not well. Public opinion was turning against slavery. It was no bad thing that Bristol was fast relinquishing the profitable commerce in human beings to Liverpool, its young and pushing rival in the north; Bristol would get on very well without that. But the plantations, they were saying, could not compete in world markets without slave labour. If slavery were outlawed, what would become of the West Indies trade? More important still, what would happen if protection were removed and cheap refined sugar from Europe flooded the country? It might have been better, he thought, if Bristol merchants had spread their risks far and wide as they had always done before Cabot sailed down the Avon to find a new westward route to Cathay and found the New World instead.

And now the war cast its shadow over all. England's back was to the wall and the French triumphed everywhere. Merchant ships, unless armed, dare not sail the Atlantic except in convoy, and even the Channel and Biscay—the route from the wine countries—were desperately unsafe. At home the price of bread was high, and there was unrest among the poor. The gentry, hard hit by taxation, would soon perhaps be buying less wine. The duty had gone up last year and was likely, they said, to go up again.

Bristol port was handling more goods than ever before. But there was room for improvement there. The close corporation which controlled the docks was conservative and seemed to consider only immediate profit. It had raised port dues so high that some trade was shifting to Liverpool. And it would not spend money on modernization—a floating harbour, for instance. It was a scandal in these days to see those fine Bristol-built ships wallowing like hogs on the mud at low tide. The name of "Bristol hog" ought to be a thing of the past.

Perry took a deep breath and raised his eyes to the busy scene before him. It was a fine sight after all. There had always been pessimists and croakers. He remembered being told that thirteen years ago, when the American colonies were only recently lost, John Pretor Pinney—a West Indies merchant, too, who should have known better—had proclaimed England's ruin: "Alas! I am afraid her Sun is set, to rise no more." England's sun had not set. Bristol, to which the American trade had meant so much, had shifted its chief effort to the West Indies and prospered more than before. Bristol would always recover. There was an obstinate spirit here which, given time, would overcome every setback.

The wine trade, too, had a vitality of its own. Through centuries of war, piracy, taxation and a hundred misfortunes it had survived and grown. It was always adapting itself. There had been a time when wine, in England, meant little else but the mild, young beverage wines of Gascony. Now, how much French wine came in? A little claret and burgundy for connoisseurs, champagne for the aristocracy and the new rich. But look at those casks piled on the quay. All port and sherry. These were the things today for a provincial merchant like himself. He was going to pin his faith on the wines of the Peninsula where Bristol men had had the closest, most continuous ties for many centuries.

His business, and that solid old house in Denmark Street, and the port of Bristol with which his fortunes were bound up—what was in store for them? How would they stand in twenty years' time, in a hundred or a hundred and fifty years? Only the future could tell.

A man crossed the gangplank of one of the ships and strode towards Perry, while a brawny sailor followed carrying a sea-chest. The blue coat with shining buttons and the buckled shoes showed a man of substance; the firm step and square shoulders spoke of authority easily carried. Making for Hanover Street nearby, he passed so close that Perry saw the glint in dark eyes under thick black brows and a hint of humour at the corners of a firm mouth. That was young Thomas Harvey, master of the *Hector*. Perry had seen in *Felix Farley's Journal* the notice of her arrival from Jamaica with the usual cargo—sugar, rum, coffee, logwood and fustic for dyes. He knew the man and his father, old Thomas Harvey of the foghorn voice, by reputation; as tough a pair of sea dogs as any in the port. They sailed John Maxse's best ships to the Indies and neither hurricanes nor Frenchmen had ever stopped them. The *Hector* had crossed in convoy this year; but it was rumoured that Maxse and Harvey were applying for letters of marque so that they could arm her and fend for themselves; the convoys were too slow for their liking. That was the proper spirit if Bristol was to survive and prosper in these times.

What had the Harveys to do with William Perry and the future of his business? A great deal in fact; but he could not know that. He forgot them and returned to his speculations. He thought now of the past. This vast commerce that carried the products of Bristol and western England to the Baltic, Iceland, America, Africa, India and the Far East; and this age-old, prosperous trade in wine from foreign lands —how had it all come about? He stood there alone on the quay with his back to Denmark Street, watching and wondering.

PART I

RETROSPECT

CHÂTEAU LATOUR

CHAPTER I

Origins

IF William Perry could have been transported back through
more than seven hundred years to the time of the Con-
queror, not only the ships but the river itself would have
vanished from before his eyes, leaving only an expanse
of marsh from the foot of the hill to the distant Avon, beyond
which was the red cliff, as yet crowned by no great church.
The Frome, instead of flowing past him towards his right,
turned away across the marsh on his left to join the loop of the
Avon well above the red cliff, so that the town stood—a
group of tiled and thatched houses crowded within its wall—
almost completely enclosed by two rivers.

Its name was Bricgstow. It was Bristow until quite recent
times. Bristolians today have a trick of speech which gives to
words ending in a vowel-sound a final 'l'. America, for
instance, becomes Americal. In the same way Bristow has
been transformed into Bristol.

Bricgstow means "bridge place". Possession of a bridge
was a distinction in Anglo-Saxon times. Bristol owed its
importance to this, to its position at the gateway to the west,
and to the long navigable reach of the Avon which offered
ships comparative safety from seaborne enemies. From the
first it was a place of trade. How far its ships had ventured
before the Conquest, or with what merchandise they were
laden, we do not know, except that they carried on a flourishing commerce with the Norsemen who occupied Ireland, and
that slaves were the mainstay of this trade. In the town
market it was a common sight to see ranks of men and women,
bound together with ropes, exposed for sale.

Whether wine was coming to Bristol before the Conquest
is not known. It was certainly coming to England. Perhaps
the Phoenician traders from Tyre, who visited our shores
long before the Romans, brought cargoes of wine from the

23

sunny south to exchange for English wool and tin. The
Romans were fond of their luxuries and were unlikely to go
without them during a spell of duty on the mist-bound island
in the far corner of their empire. The Saxons too were familiar
with wine; to them it was a drink, a medicine and an instrument of magic.

Whatever its early history, wine in England was put on a
new footing by Christianity. (That is, by the country's
conversion to the Roman Church under St. Augustine.
There was a church in Britain before that: and perhaps, if
the beautiful Glastonbury legend is true, the first of all
Christian Churches was founded in western England by
Joseph of Arimathea himself.) Augustine and his missionaries
brought with them the strict rules of Rome, one of which for-
bade the use in the communion of any liquid other than the
juice of the grape; so wine now had a religious status.

The bringers of continental Christianity also brought continental tastes, and closer contact with Europe caused a
revival of trade in general. So it came about that wine was
being imported on a fair scale before the Norman Conquest.
French wines came through Rouen, which had its own land-
ing-place, Dunegate, or Dowgate, on the Thames. (The name
is preserved by Dowgate Hill, off Cannon Street, in the City.)
It is probable also that Lorraine ships were bringing wine of
the Rhine to London Bridge.

The Church brought to England not only wine in greater
quantity, but the vine itself. The monks of the early abbeys
—chief centres of husbandry as of learning and the crafts—
planted vines and made wine from the grapes they grew.
Perhaps the soil was more suitable then to the growth of the
grape; this is almost certainly true of parts of northern
France. At all events, quality was not the first consideration;
the wine was not meant to be drunk for pleasure. Later,
vineyards became the fashion among a few rich landowners.
A twelfth-century writer records that Gloucestershire was
reputed to produce the best wine grapes; *Domesday Book*
mentions a vineyard near Stonehouse; and today a wood near
Aust, a few miles from Bristol, preserves in its name, the
Vineyard, a record of its past.

Under Norman Rule

Bristol did not resist the Norman conquerors of England. This was not owing to lack of spirit, for the following year, when a son of Earl Harold brought a force from Ireland and attacked the town in the hope of plunder, he got such a reception as sent him away disappointed and empty handed. It was owing to the citizens' commercial instincts; they tended to regard a stranger, in default of evidence to the contrary, as someone to trade with, not as an enemy. And indeed Norman rule brought them much benefit. The castle which rose to cast its massive shadow on the neck of their peninsula was a symbol of law and order; the roads were safer to travel; and the Norman barons with their large, migrant retinues set a new standard of hospitality. All this was good for trade and for the wine trade in particular.

So wine became plentiful in England, and the traveller could be more confident of getting it at a wayside inn than he would be today.

He would pay about a penny a gallon for it—more after poor vintages, less after good. It was not of course at that time, or for many centuries after, the choice, long-matured product that comes from the modern cellar. It was imported and kept in the cask, and drunk in its first year.

By the twelfth century, wine was coming to Bristol port in substantial quantities. There is a reference to this in the city's archives today, in the record of a dispute which arose three centuries later, in the reign of Henry VI, concerning the "prise"—the customary right of kings to take a part of every ship's cargo. The prior of St. James's Priory stated in evidence that the prise during Whit Week had been given to his predecessor by William, Earl of Gloucester, in the time of Stephen, so that the holders of his office 1422–61

> . . . from time out of mind, have had and have been accustomed to have from any ships coming to the aforesaid port of Bristol in the week of Pentecost, from twelve o'clock on Saturday, the vigil of Pentecost, to the same hour on the following Saturday right prisage of wines. . . .

(The prior won his case, and so the monks continued to enjoy their ancient privilege.)

The men of Bristol had given up their traffic in slaves,

persuaded by the good Bishop Wulfstan's long campaign of preaching. But their link with Ireland remained: Scandinavia too was now within their orbit, and goods in greater variety travelled up and down the Avon and across the sea. Merchants from other English towns and from abroad flocked to the great St. James's Day Fair, to buy Cotswold cloth, leather from tanneries beside the Avon, Bristol-made soap, and goods carried from abroad to Bristol port. A twelfth-century writer praised "the famous town of Bristow" and its harbour, a commodious and safe refuge for ships from "outlandish and foreign" countries, where the commodities of other lands were exchanged for those of Bristol and its surrounding districts—a region fortunate and blessed with the riches of nature.

1135–54 Another described it as it was in the reign of King Stephen, a "most opulent city", with a tidal harbour able to receive a thousand ships (his enthusiasm no doubt led him to exaggerate). The whole town, he wrote, seems to float upon the waters and to be seated on their banks.

Thus blessed in their port and its surroundings, and absorbed in their prosperous commerce, the men of Bristol were not without warlike impulses. During Stephen's reign they kidnapped the Bishop of Bath and others of the king's supporters and held them to ransom; and the burgesses of Marlborough were glad to pay for King John's protection against their attacks. Meanwhile, the town was suffering from growing pains. It stretched out westward across the marsh and southward beyond the Avon to Temple Meads (meads then, now site of the city's main railway station) and to meet its rival Redcliff.

A Momentous Marriage

1154–89 Henry II's marriage to Eleanor of Aquitaine added to England's continental possessions many of the finest wine-growing districts of France. The wines of Aquitaine were already favoured in England: now they took first place. The province of Gascony, finding the English market open and eager, was encouraged to specialize in the production of wines, and these—handled hitherto by Rouen like other French wines—were henceforth shipped to England from Gascony's own port, Bordeaux. The Bordeaux merchants formed their own federation in London, where they were welcomed as English subjects; in time more than one of them became mayor of the city. For centuries most of the wine drunk in England came from Gascony. Later there was a long succession of tragic happenings; but never, from that day to this, has claret—the name of the red wines shipped from Bordeaux—been without its loyal supporters among Englishmen of taste.

Though Bristol sailors were familiar with the western coasts of Europe, they did not at that time bring much wine from Bordeaux. The carrying trade was mainly in foreign hands. The merchants of the town were generally content to have their wine brought to them, provided that no stranger might sell ashore. When a wine ship from Bordeaux or elsewhere berthed in the docks, they would go aboard and buy what they wanted for their cellars: they were vintners rather than shippers. Nevertheless, it was geography that traced the line between these two great ports and brought the rich gifts of Gascony to the western half of England, via the Avon.

The English possessions in France led to disputes between the two countries, and to war. By the end of John's reign most of them were lost. The Gascon trade and the link with Bordeaux became all the more important to England, and to Bristol. In spite of this there was jealousy between English and Gascon merchants. In the reign of Edward I foreign ships and cargoes were seized in English ports and sometimes their crews were murdered. Bristol, however, if it took part in these affairs at all, was less inhospitable than London, where the City authorities so oppressed foreign merchants that much of the Bordeaux trade was diverted to other ports; and Bristol and Hull, the leading provincial wine ports, reaped most of the benefit.

1199–1216

1272–1307

The New Quay

In the early part of the thirteenth century Bristol's only accommodation for ships was on the Avon. By 1250 there was a fine new quay within sight of the place where William Perry has been standing all this time. The townsmen had purchased from the abbot of St. Augustine's a strip of marshland, and through this they had carved a new, wide channel for the Frome, starting where its old course began to curve

away towards the Avon, and joining the larger river nearly
half a mile farther south, between its sharp westward curve
and the point where it passes the great gateway of St.
Vincent's Rocks and plunges into the spectacular Avon
Gorge. It was a great work for those times, costing £5,000.
The new quay was built on the bank of this channel at the
place called St. Augustine's Back; and here the ships came
from Ireland and Scandinavia, France, Portugal and Spain.
For smaller vessels of the Welsh and coastwise trade there
was another quay, the Welsh Back, on the Avon below the
bridge.

Now the people of Bristol pulled down the old bridge and
built in its place, to connect the original town with its out-
growths towards Temple and Redcliff, a fine new one of
stone, with four arches, carrying tall houses over the water
on either side of the roadway like the famous Old London
Bridge, and shops beneath them.

In the fourteenth century Bristol became a county,
separated both from Gloucestershire and Somerset. In its
1327–77 archives today is the beautiful charter by which Edward III
granted this privilege in 1373,

> . . . noting that it is a long way for the burgesses of Bristol to
> attend county courts etc. at Gloucester or Ilchester . . . and also
> in consideration of the good behaviour of the said burgesses
> towards us and of their good services given us in times past by
> their shipping and other things and for six hundred marks
> which they have paid to us ourselves into our Chamber.

By the end of that century Bristol was the leading port of the
west of England and one of the three greatest in the kingdom,
rivalling Hull for first place, after London, in the wine trade.
As to the size of its population there is no very sound evidence,
but it was almost certainly well under 10,000 souls. Yet this
would be a high figure for that rural age when many important
towns were less than 3,000. Apart from London, probably
only York, Norwich and Coventry—all rival cloth towns—
could claim to be as large or larger.

How Wine was Handled

What happened when a wine ship berthed at the new quay
on St. Augustine's Back? If we may judge from the ordinances applying in London during the thirteenth and fourteenth

centuries, the handling of wine was under careful control. There at least every cargo was first inspected, then landed under the auspices of the Corporation of Wine Drawers, who were solemnly sworn to perform their office faithfully and well. Each cask was gauged by royal officers to ensure that it contained the proper quantity, and then sold by appointed brokers who were sworn-in like the drawers. There were customs collectors, and controllers to watch the collectors, and searchers with keen noses to smell out attempted customs evasions. Either before or after landing a representative of the king's butler came to take the prise—one tun from a cargo of less than twenty tuns; two from a cargo of twenty tuns or more, one from before the mast and one from aft. This was an anxious time for the merchants, for the official might have instructions, under the royal right of purveyance, to take more than the prise; and, though he was supposed to pay for what he took or to give written promise of payment, this part of the proceedings was sometimes omitted. Apart from what was required for the king's table and the royal household, huge quantities were sometimes requisitioned for the troops. Once in the reign of Richard II the bailiffs of Bristol had orders 1377–99 that no tavern might receive wine but all must go to the army.

The prise itself, or part of it, was sometimes assigned to some beneficiary. We have quoted as an instance the monks of St. James's Priory. Later, Bristol had orders from Edward III that one-third of the prise was to go to Queen 1327–77 Philippa, and six tuns every year to a lady named Joan de Carrue, whose claim to the privilege is not known.

The retail trade (here again we are quoting the London ordinances) was just as carefully supervised. Taverns were watched, and there were strict measures to prevent the mixing of good and bad, or even good wines of different origins. Sour liquor must be thrown away. One offender convicted of selling bad wine was made to drink as much of it as he could hold, and what was left was poured over his head.

There was evidently need for vigilance. The tricks to which vintners, coopers and foreign merchants resorted are set forth in an ordinance preserved at the London Guildhall, ascribed to the year 1419. It describes how "bothe Englishmen and aliens in comone harme of all the Peple and gret sclaundre of the Citee" are in the habit of treating wines of

Spain and Rochelle and other "remenauntz of brokyn sodyn reboyllid and unthrifty wynes of other contrees" so as to make them resemble Romeney in colour and taste, and further many such wines are "deceyvablych contrefetyd and medlid on the other syde of the sea and broght hydir to selle". The mayor and aldermen have accordingly ordained that no man shall sell such counterfeit Romeney for more than 6*d.* per gallon, nor mix white with red, old with new, etc., on pain of the pillory.

Glass bottles did not exist at this time. Wine remained in the cask until it was drawn into jugs to be carried to the table. The secrets of keeping and maturing were unknown. When 1212–72 Henry III gave orders to clear old stocks from his Bristol cellars to make room for the new vintage, he was following the normal practice: for wine that had been kept a year was past its best. Such stuff might be re-exported: in 1400 one Thomas Clerk, master of *La Trinité* of Bristol, was licensed to carry to Ireland twenty tuns of old wine which could not be sold in England. Either the Irish were less particular, or this wine was destined for use as vinegar.

Besides the wines of Gascony, small quantities came to England from northern and southern France, Italy and the eastern Mediterranean. The sunny southern wines—Languedoc, Cyprus, Crete, Muscadell, Tyre—though still a novelty and a luxury, were important enough by the fourteenth century to be classed separately under the style of "sweet" wines. Wines of Spain and Portugal—though they did not at all resemble the works of art which we know today as sherry and port—were held in high esteem; and it is likely that Bristol merchants handled a large share of them along with the fruit, Seville oil, white Castile soap, iron, goatskins and woad which they exchanged for west of England cloth and fish from the north Atlantic.

From the thirteenth century onwards English merchants were sending their own ships in increasing numbers to bring wine from Gascony each autumn. One writer says that there were two hundred British ships loading wine at Bordeaux in 1372; though this may be an exaggeration it at least suggests a respectable number. Many ports on the east, south and west coasts were active in the trade, but none except London and possibly Hull could compare with Bristol.

The broad, blunt-ended "cog" with a single square sail which was the regular ship of burden at this time, was a stout little craft. As portrayed in the margins of manuscripts and in carvings and stained glass windows, it looks hardly sea-worthy—high in the water, with cumbrous erections on bow and stern. Yet it braved the storms of Biscay and generally survived, although certainly many were lost. The largest recorded before 1400 were 300 tuns, but some as small as 15 to 20 tuns were known to leave their edging round the coast and venture on the voyage to Bordeaux.

Hazards

In 1214 the reeves of Bristol were ordered to produce a list of all vessels belonging to the port which could carry 80 tuns of wine or more: an ominous sign. Disputes, resentments and hostilities between England and France clouded the following two and a half centuries, culminating in the Hundred Years 1339–1453 War. Many Bristol ships were pressed into service, to carry troops to France or to help protect English shores or convoys. They made an important contribution; but the unfortunate owners lost their freights and often their ships, and were lucky if they got any compensation. Even those who were allowed to keep their vessels in trade had their troubles. If they sailed in convoy (which was made compulsory at intervals from 1336 onwards) they had to pay a subsidy of two or three shillings a tun for naval protection. In any case merchant ships were themselves equipped for self-defence. A comple-ment of armed men must be provided and paid, and the cumbersome "castles" fore and aft became more solid and permanent. Besides the cost, the added weight decreased the vessel's pay-load. Insurance rates increased. The freight from Bordeaux to Bristol was about 8*s*. per tun at the beginning of the fourteenth century: in 1372 it was 22*s*.

Meanwhile the war came to Gascony. Many of its rich vineyards were ravaged, and famine and pestilence followed. Each year in the early part of the fourteenth century, except those affected by the war, 90,000 or 100,000 tuns of wine had been shipped abroad from Bordeaux and other ports of western France; of this nearly a quarter came to England, and Bristol's share was often over 3,000 tuns. The retail price in England was between 3*d*. and 4*d*. a gallon. Each fresh outbreak of war or pestilence produced a setback; peace and good vintages were followed by recovery.

Although damage could not be quickly repaired, the trade showed amazing vitality in face of such hardships. Yet production inevitably dropped. By the end of the century Gascony's exports were a fraction of what they had been; and, although England was now taking almost all, its imports were less than the pre-war figure. With higher prices in Gascony and increased freight rates, Gascon wine was never again so cheap nor so abundant in England as it had been.

The war continued until 1453. At least there was no real peace, but continual pillage and plunder on both sides. No sea captain knew what ship might attack him, and few were scrupulous as to whom they attacked; and the courts were hard put to it to administer justice when vessels of friendly or neutral nations were the victims. We have records of several such cases. In 1403 Castile sued for restitution of seven ships alleged to have been captured by an English fleet of which Thomas Norton, a well-known Bristol merchant, was one of the commanders. (His colleague was John Hawley, of Dartmouth, who had often been appointed to officiate in the investigation of acts of piracy!) In another case Henry May, owner of the *Trinity* of Bristol, rescued a Portuguese ship from pirates, but, when he found that the pirates were English, he left the Portuguese to their fate. A third was brought before the Chancellor by a Bordeaux citizen, Barnard Bensyn, who said he had consigned 10 tuns of red wine to Ireland in the *Bartilmewe* of Bristol, and paid the owner, Barnard Brennyng, 3s. 3d. "in earnest and in binding thereof"; but Brennyng took the wine to Bristol and there converted it to his own use.

English ships were the victims as often as they were the aggressors. John Wyche of Bristol filled both roles in quick succession. While fishing off Ireland in 1449 in his ship the *Mary* he captured a Spanish vessel laden with wine, iron and salt; whereupon certain Irishmen of Kinsale—so Wyche alleged in his petition to the Chancellor—manned "diverse vessels", slew three of the *Mary*'s crew and took the Spaniard and her freight away.

The voyage from Bordeaux was beset from end to end by pirates—Spanish, Breton and English too. Bristol men themselves were not guilty of piracy, at this time at least, to the same extent as those of the south coast from the Cinque Ports to Cornwall. Geography limited their opportunities for rapid foray.

In face of such hazards ships struggled through with the new vintage every autumn. The risks were great, but so were the rewards; and the sailors were bold and resolute men. Yet it is no wonder that a fraternity was founded in Marsh Street (in the seamen's quarter which had grown up on the marsh around the old course of the Frome) in 1445 to pray for the souls of merchants and mariners at sea.

In 1453 the French took Bordeaux. The war was over, but not the bitterness. King Edward IV—resolved apparently 1461-83 to hurt those who were still England's friends if he could not damage her enemies—prohibited all imports from the lost provinces. Bristol suffered; but, because its ventures were spread wide, it suffered far less than Gascony, which was now almost entirely dependent on its wine production and the English market. Yet the Gascony trade was never quite destroyed. Commerce, founded on goodwill and mutual benefit, has a sturdy resilience. England still loved the "mighty great" wines of Gascony, and some still came in by devious channels, defeating the ban. The Bordeaux merchants still looked to England; they could scarcely do otherwise. Barnard Bensyn, in spite of the grievance expressed in his petition, was so attached (by interest perhaps rather than sentiment) to Bristol that he came and settled there; and so did a number of his fellow citizens. The tomb of one of them, William Lombard, can still be seen in St. Nicholas' Church, and his will is preserved in the city's archives. As soon as the first bitterness of defeat died down the Gascony trade began to revive. After the treaty of 1475—although King Richard III complained to Louis of France that his subjects 1483-85 "dare not venture to Bordeaux"—the exchange of Gascon wine for west of England broadcloth was once more proceeding briskly through Bristol port.

CHAPTER II

Trade before Politics

THROUGHOUT the fifteenth century Bristol merchants found golden opportunities in spite of war with France and the civil strife which followed it; and those who were both determined and lucky built up solid fortunes. In the latter part of the century their ships were visiting most parts of northern Europe as far as Bergen, entering the Baltic, and twice braving the jealousy of Italian merchant cities, attempting to reach the Levant, though each voyage ended in disaster. But their main routes radiated westward—to Ireland, the Atlantic coasts of France, Spain and Portugal, and now to Iceland, which was soon to lead them yet farther west. Geography was still playing a part in shaping the destiny of Bristol.

The rich inland area which it served contributed to the town's wealth. Wool was carried from as far as Buckingham, Coventry, Hereford and Wales to be spun and woven in the villages of the Cotswolds and Mendips, whose fine churches, built with money earned by wool, were hung with bells cast in Bristol foundries; and the cloth was finished in a new suburb south of the Avon, where in Touker Street—street of the tuckers or fullers—lengths of fulled cloth hung drying on the tenters, and dyed pieces added bright patches of colour. Cornish tin, hides from west Wales, and timber and iron from the Forest of Dean supplied other Bristol industries. Down the Severn from Gloucester and Worcester corn was brought, not only for export, but also to feed the town's growing industrial population. Sculptured alabaster came from Coventry and Nottingham to enrich its churches and, by export, foreign churches as far apart as Iceland and Portugal. With all these English towns there was a brisk exchange of trade, in which wine had its part. It travelled up the Severn into Shropshire, and down the Bristol Channel to Barnstaple.

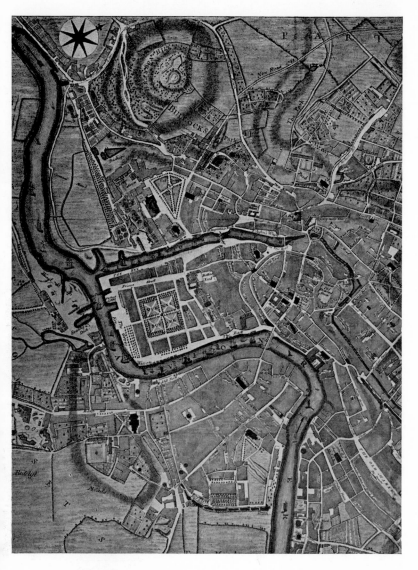

2   A map of Bristol in 1780 by R. Benning. Denmark Street, site of the
firm's premises since 1796, may be seen as a curved street running down
to the River Frome, south of the drawbridge. The Lord Mayor's Chapel,
     facing College Green, is immediately behind Denmark Street

3   The quayside at Bordeaux
From an early eighteenth-century engraving

4   Oporto in the nineteenth century
From a contemporary painting

Englishmen now had a greater variety of wines to choose from. Malmsey, a name for the various growths of Crete, was becoming famous. Crete was under the sway of Venice, and almost all the trade of the eastern Mediterranean (which sent many wines to England besides Malmsey) was controlled by the rich merchant cities of Italy. They guarded it jealously, as Robert Sturmy learned when, on his second attempt to reach the Levant in 1457, his ship was destroyed off Malta by the Genoese. The Italians were glad enough to sell their wares in England, provided they carried them thither themselves. They rarely came to Bristol, preferring the shorter journey to the south coast ports. This did not prevent their trading with Bristol merchants, who used some of these ports, as they used London also, carrying their purchases the rest of the way by land. From Southampton records we know the names of various Bristol men who traded in this way and the nature of the goods they handled—most often a very mixed bag, though wine was generally included. One day in 1449, for instance, six wagons set out from Southampton for Bristol and two for Salisbury laden with merchandise from southern Europe—wine, raisins, herrings, black soap, alum, almonds and wax; all the property of Nicholas Lange of Bristol.

This overland trade was a matter of convenience, no doubt, and another instance of the effects of geography. The lack of direct and friendly contact with the Italians may have caused in Bristol a certain coldness towards them compared with its long and close relations with the people of Spain. So at least it appears from the case of a Genoese merchant, Nicholas de Brignali. He and some compatriots consigned a cargo of wine, oil and other merchandise to Southampton or alternatively to the Thames. The master of the ship, who was a Spaniard, sailed instead to Bristol—so Nicholas alleged in his petition to the Chancellor—"against his promise and contrary to all faith and conscience"; and, though the owners produced a warrant from their sovereign for the arrest of the ship and its master, the mayor and other officers and merchants of the town "oweth the nation of Spain so great love and affiance" that they proposed not only to let the ship and cargo remain at Bristol but to make Nicholas pay for the freight thither.

As the merchants of the late fifteenth century pushed their

ventures farther across the seas, Bristol shipyards built them larger and better ships, with two or even three masts and a greater expanse of sail. More ships too; for an owner, whose father had probably been content with a part share in one vessel, might now control a little fleet of his own. As their wealth increased they built luxurious houses for themselves and enriched their beloved city by improving and adding to its churches.

Most famous of them all was William Canynges. His father and grandfather had founded a solid fortune on cloth and shipping. William himself, a shipowner pure and simple, amassed great wealth from freights. A writer of his day listed nine ships which Canynges owned—a tenth had been lost off Iceland—and gave the displacement of the largest, the *Mary and John*, as 900 tuns; a remarkable figure if it is true.

Canynges' name is associated with the finest of all Bristol churches, St. Mary Redcliff, in the district which was his home for most of his life. The work—in fact the reconstruction and improvement of an older church—was begun by his grandfather: William carried it on and then, after the spire collapsed, largely rebuilt it.

He was five times mayor of the town. After his last term of office in 1466 he immediately retired from the world and took orders in the collegiate church of Westbury. He managed to combine piety and conviviality in a high degree, and showed his generous spirit in small things as well as in great. It is recorded that he gave 190 gallons of wine at his own expense to be distributed to the Crafts at the midsummer watch.

It is worth noting how easily Canynges turned from the temporal to the eternal—from building a ship to rebuilding a church, from the mayor's office to holy orders. This spirit was natural then, and gave a zest and brightness to life which makes one regret its loss. But, in Canynges, there is something particular which is part of the character of Bristol men; a combination of commercial hard-headedness with an occasional dream, a capacity at times to see things distant and immaterial; unexpected and disconcerting to strangers, yet strikingly in keeping with the scenery and surroundings of the place. It appeared in later generations too.

1455–85   The Wars of the Roses were mainly the concern of noble families, who spent on them their fortunes and their blood.

The merchants of Bristol were more interested in the brightening prospect of trade than in disputes for possession of the English crown; and, whatever happened to their rivals in other towns, they came through this troubled time more prosperous than ever. It was a period of expansion for the middle class, who lived more lavishly in proportion to their growing fortunes. But, unlike the feudal nobles and lords of the church, they had not yet begun to lay down private cellars. They purchased their wine piecemeal, and very often consumed it in the tavern. There they met their friends and found a congenial atmosphere, half public, half intimate—the prototype nearly 500 years ago of the English inn.

An Expanding World

Up and down the western coasts from the Peninsula to Iceland, in harbours opening on the broad Atlantic, there were stories—part tradition, part fairy-tale—of mysterious lands beyond the ocean, full of gold and spices and peopled by demons and strange beasts. These legends travelled, along with cargoes of fish and wine and oil, to Bristol quay. In the sailormen's taverns around Marsh Street and St. Augustine's Back, and in the rich houses of the merchants, they found receptive ears and hearts always ready to respond to their double message—the promise of new wealth, and the hint of improbable romance. As early as 1480 John Jay and his company sailed two ships out of Kingroad, the Avon anchorage, to look for "the Island of Brasylle to the West of Ireland". They did not find it. But their attempt was the prelude to great things: for Bristol men were still fascinated by Brazil and the "Seven Cities". They listened to the persuasive voice of Cabot—an Italian by birth, a citizen of Bristol by adoption—who in 1497 took a Bristol ship and a crew of West Country men across the Atlantic and planted the English flag in the soil of the New World.

It is an odd fact that America was discovered under a misapprehension. The object of all early exploration westward was to find a new route to the fabulous wealth of the East, and Cabot himself imagined that he had reached the territory of the "Grand Cham", the Emperor of China. It was none the less a glorious feat, and it stirred ambition in others. "There is no land uninhabitable or sea unnavigable,"

1509–47 a Bristol man, one of the Thornes, wrote to Henry VIII a
generation later. The world was expanding. The period
covered by Tudor rule in England, which had its climax in
the glorious reign of Elizabeth I, was a new era, the era of the
Renaissance. Men were looking outwards. They saw a larger
world—new knowledge, new lands, new power over things if
not over themselves; more money to be had, more goods to
spend it on. Perhaps they did not see so clearly that an
expanding world implied new national rivalries and new
strains and stresses in the social fabric. When Englishmen
fixed their ambitions on the New World and on maritime
expansion elsewhere, they were setting themselves up in
competition with two great navigator nations, Spain and
Portugal.

Trade was the root of the quarrel. England wanted new
markets for the increasing products of industry; and English
sailors, who saw no reason why they should not sail every
ocean as they pleased and reap the rewards of adventure,
defied the dictates of the Pope who had allotted the East
Indies to Portugal and the West Indies to Spain. The result
was pillage and murder wherever the ships of the rival
countries met; and Bristol men, whose fortunes were founded
on trade and industry, were as much involved as any.

It was not until the 1540's that such acts became general.
Before that the Peninsular trade was flourishing. In the reign
1485–1509 of Henry VII there were many Bristol merchants resident in
Lisbon, and at least one Bristol mercantile family, the
Thornes, had agents in Spain and the Spanish territories
early in the sixteenth century. England's imports of
Spanish wines were beginning to overhaul those from
Bordeaux, and the name of sack became known for the first
time. Even later, the ties of friendship and mutual interest
were almost as strong as the impulses of rivalry and plunder.
The company trading with Spain and Portugal had seventy-
six Bristol members in 1577—far more than from any other
town except London. In this same year, the Town Clerk
wrote in *The Mayor of Bristow's Calendar*, "came from
Andoluzia suche sweete and pleasant secks in generall as by
reporte the like was neuer knowen".

On the other hand there were many Bristol men among
those who took delight in harrying the Spanish argosies; and

others were provoked to revenge by the high-handed actions of the dons. In 1576 Andrew Barker, who traded in cloth and wine between Bristol and the Canaries, had all his goods in Teneriffe, to the value of £1,700, seized and his factor imprisoned by the Inquisition. He fitted out two barques and sailed on a voyage of reprisal, attacking Spanish ships along the Caribbean coast. His crews mutinied and he was caught and killed on an island in the Bay of Honduras by a Spanish frigate; whereupon the captain of Barker's second vessel took the Spaniard and sailed her to England with a treasure worth £2,000.

So the two countries continued in a doubtful relationship, influenced both by mutual interest and enmity. In time the balance swung towards war.

In Bristol Public Library is a copy of an old book, *The Marchants Avizo* (it is dedicated to Thomas Aldworth, Mayor of Bristol, and to "all the worshipfull company of the Merchants of the said City"), which contains a poem written in 1587, "when was a long stay of the Merchants trade, to the great decay of many a one". The first two verses read:

> When Merchants trade proceeds in peace,
>   And labours prosper well:
> Then Common-weales in wealth increase,
>   As now good proofe can tell.
>
> For when the Merchants trade was free,
>   His ventures for to make:
> Then every Arte in his degree
>   Some gaines thereof did take. . . .

Then came the Armada. Bristol's contribution to the fleet which met the attack was a modest one—three ships and a pinnace. Eight years later, when John Hopkins, fishmonger and mayor of the city, returned from taking part with his own ship in the expedition to Cadiz, he was given a joyful reception on Durdham Down, and the citizens lighted "all their tallow candells, and a great bonfire at the High Crosse, very beautifull to beholde".

Still, many Bristol hearts must have been sore to see hostility growing towards their best customer, and a country where some of them spent a great part of their lives.

In fact this long war never quite destroyed trade; some Spanish wine was always coming to England through neutral channels, and it seems that Bristol was a favourite port of entry. In 1597 Thomas Honyman of London sent his clerk to St. Malo to see what he could get, and received from him this note:

> I will stay a little longer to see what can be done, and wait the coming of the ships out of Spain, which are daily expected with good wine, and send it to Bristol, a better place for them than London.

Portugal, involved perforce in the war on the Spanish side, continued to send its wine ships direct to England in spite of all risks.

Yet inevitably war did great damage to the trade as a whole. England's wine imports, which had more than doubled during Henry VII's reign and climbed still higher in the early 1558-1603 years of Elizabeth I, were down by a third before 1600, when sweet wine was selling at 4s. a gallon and Gascon at 2s. 8d. (This is in London: prices were higher in inland towns.) It was no wonder that merchants sighed for peace.

Wine and its Rivals in Tudor England

The wines of Gascony were still popular in England. In 1509-47 the early part of Henry VIII's reign, in addition to the normal trade, many persons, including some Bristol merchants, were given special licences to import from Bordeaux.

There was a minor setback when King Francis offended His Majesty of England by showing reluctance to assist in his search for yet another wife: he was not prepared "to bring ladies of high rank like geldings to market". Henry's attitude to France and things French changed abruptly; he said "he would rather drink beer, or even water, than allow his subjects to import French wines as abundantly as they used in former times", and imposed restrictions on imports from France which fortunately proved impossible to enforce. Yet these good wines, which had once been so plentiful and so cheap, were becoming scarce. About the middle of the century a Venetian ambassador in London, reporting on English drinking habits, mentioned in particular the wines of "Candia,

Spain, the Rhine, and from France, this last being valued more than the rest, but it is sold at a very high price". He also noted of beer: "This potion is most palatable to them, and all persons drink it, even their Sovereigns." Elizabeth I took notice of "the great and excessive prices of wines of the growing of the realm of France", and tried to improve the situation by allowing all persons of any friendly country to bring these wines to England provided they paid the customs and duties due.

The mentions of beer are significant. When Henry VIII entertained the French queen in 1518 the party consumed 3 tuns and 2 pieces of wine, which were charged in the expenses at £13 3s. 4d., and 6 tuns and 7 hogsheads of ale, which were charged at £7 14s. 2d.

If kings and nobles consumed beer in such quantities when wine was also on the table, it is likely that the lower classes were developing a preference for the cheaper drink. It is true that troops on active service still expected to be supplied with wine: but it was less plentiful than of old. The soldiers sent to France by Henry VIII to help the Emperor's invasion had "to go three or four days without drinking anything but water, a sort of privation which military men seldom endure without falling into despair". But rising prices were turning them to drinks less expensive than wine. *Adam's Chronicle of Bristol* records that the English troops in Portugal in 1589, having thrown away their pikes and arquebuses in order to carry looted wine, "by means thereof fell into divers diseases and died in great numbers, the English nation not being accustomed to drink wine always, and their beer is not so strong a kind of drink".

Wine had other competitors, some of them less innocuous than beer. Spirits were known in England even in the Middle Ages—*usquebaugh* from Ireland, *aqua vitae* from Spain and France, the originals of whisky and brandy respectively. Home distilling was first established by the monks, the chief exponents of so many arts and crafts. The early history of spirits was, on the whole, thoroughly respectable; they were used largely for medicine. But now there came a change—not in the merits of the thing itself, but in the use people made of it. In 1585 Elizabeth I sent an expedition to the Low Countries. There, as in Germany, drinking was a serious matter, and spirits were the most effective passport to the status and condition of a superman.

The sociable Dutch initiated English soldiers into the mysteries of real, deliberate drunkenness; they learnt the lesson, brought it home, and spread it. Before the end of the century distilleries in England were making *aqua vitae* in large quantities: and in order to meet the demand for cheap spirits they were distilling, it is stated, not only wine and wine lees, but hogwash and such-like materials.

The number of drinking houses was increasing enormously. 1547–53 Edward VI, in an effort to control the "many tavernes of late newly sette uppe in very great noumbre in backe lanes, corners and suspicious places within the Cytie of London, and in divers other townes and vyllages within this Realme", fixed a limit to the number permitted—40 for London, 8 for York, 6 for Bristol; 4, 3 or 2 for the lesser towns. But the increase continued. Elizabeth I granted licenses as she saw fit, without regard for statutes or professional qualifications. In one year Her Majesty's letter patent to retail wines in the City of London was granted, among many others, to 9 merchant tailors, 4 haberdashers, 3 fishmongers, and the widow Whittingham, of Gracechurch Street, relict of a barber-surgeon.

A Bristol Merchant

Sixteenth-century Bristol was full of solid prosperity and good cheer. It became a city in 1542 by decree of Henry VIII, and its St. James's Day Fair was described in 1576 as "not inferior to the greatest marts in Europe". Its citizens were active in exploration, attempts at colonization, the study of geography, and above all in the expansion of their trade. In fact they were as busy, as confident and adventurous as other Englishmen of their time: yet still they did things in their own way and expressed their own attitude to life.

If any one of them can be considered as typical it is John Whitson, merchant adventurer, born in 1557. We owe some particulars of Whitson to John Aubrey, who, though inaccurate in some points, was Whitson's godson and well informed on the subject in general, especially the more intimate details.

Whitson (says Aubrey)

was borne at Cover in the Forest of Deane in the Countie of
Gloucester: he went to schoole at Bristow, where he made a
good proficience in the Latin tongue. He was bound Apprentice
to Alderman Vawr, a Spanish Merchant of this City.

(Here Aubrey is wrong: Whitson was apprenticed to Nicholas
Cutts, a wine cooper and general merchant, of Nicholas
Street. But let him continue.)

He was a handsome young fellow; and his old Master (the
Alderman) being dead, his Mistress one day called him into the
Wine-celler and bad him broach the best Butt in the Cellar for
her; and truly he broach't his mistresse, who after maried him.
This story will last perhaps as long as Bristol is a City.

(Though Aubrey may have embroidered the details, the
essential fact is confirmed by the parish registers, which
record the christening of the first child only seven months
after the wedding.)

He had a very good healthy constitution and was an early
Riser; wrote all his letters and dispatched his businesse betime
in the Morning. He had a good naturall Witt, and gaind by the
Spanish trade a fair Estate. He lived nobly; kept a plentiful
table; and was the most popular magistrate in the City, alwaies
chosen a Member of Parliament. He kept a noble house, and did
entertain and treat the Peers and great Persons that came to
the City. He kept his Hawkes. . . . He settled all his Estate
upon the City of Bristow for pious Uses, and was, I doe believe,
the greatest Benefactor that ever the City had.

Another story of Whitson shows two sides of a typical
Bristol character. It relates that at one time he was concerned
as part-owner of the *Mayflowre* in privateering against
Spanish ships. When the *Mayflowre* and her companion
vessel returned to Bristol with their prizes, he noticed "many
small chests of sugar to be of severall markes, which he
judged to belong unto poor maryners to helpe theire wages, to
the reliefs of their wyves and children". His conscience smote
him; he sold his interest in the enterprise and never thereafter
would handle any prize goods.

Towards the end he turned away from the world which had
given him so much. He wrote: "Farewell Pleasures and carnal

Delights, snares to be avoided in our earthly pilgrimage; the
quick-sands whereon so many young men have suffered
shipwreck. . . ." He died, says Aubrey, about the seventy-sixth
year of his age of a fall from his horse, his head pitching on a
nail. His funeral was attended by as many poor old men
and women as he was years old in mourning gowns and
hoods.

Whitson's life was divided from Canynges' by a century
and a half; yet there are remarkable likenesses between them.
They showed a huge zest in the getting of their wealth and
the spending of it; with it they enriched and glorified their
beloved city; and then they cheerfully left both their wealth
and their sins behind them.

The same enviable ability to be on good terms with this
world and the next appears again, in a Bristol document
which has already been quoted—*The Marchants Avizo*,
written and published during Whitson's lifetime. This is
ostensibly a handbook of useful information for those engaged
in trade, "Very Necessary for their Sonnes and Servants,
When they first send them beyond the Sea, as to Spaine and
Portingale, or other Countries": but it hardly seems to distinguish between the rules for gaining advancement on earth
and in heaven; combining an earnest reminder of the "daily
duety of prayer and thanksgiving to God" with notes on the
weights and measures of Portugal, Spain and France: a
specimen bill of exchange for Spain and elsewhere; and
"Certaine godly sentences, necessary for a youth to meditate
upon", such as:

> Let not thy expenses bee equall with thy gaines: for either
> sicknesse, naughty debtors, let of trade, and misfortune by the
> sea or land, may soone overthrow thee.

Are we right in finding such a mixture incongruous? The
author of the Book of Proverbs did not think so. Nor did the
good merchants of Bristol in the fifteenth and sixteenth
centuries, nor those of the nineteenth.

To conclude; the *Avizo* has this to say about wine:

> Of Wines: it cannot be set downe by pen or words, the right
> knowledge of it, for it is perceivable onely by the taste and
> flavour. But the best sorts of wines generally are, when they

doe taste pleasant and strong withall, and when they drink
cleane and quicke in the palat of the mouth, and when they are
cleere and white hued if they be white wines, or of faire orient
red, if they bee red wines. But if they drinke weake, rough,
foule, flat, inclining to egernesse, or long: they are not good.

CHÂTEAU MARGAUX

CHAPTER III

Under the Stuarts

Bristol shipowners are very few and poor. . . . The wine trade
—one of the greatest in the city—is much impoverished. . . .
This city is poor, and insensible of any proportion with London;
two or three merchants of London are able to buy all the
inhabitants of Bristol out of their means in the world, saving
their persons. There are about 700 widows here.

1603–25   This is a harrowing picture of Bristol in the reign of James I,
but less harrowing perhaps when we know its origin. Ship
money was to be raised for an expedition against the Barbary
corsairs, and Bristol had been called on to contribute £2,500.
The Merchant Adventurers drew up a document which they
called "A Collection of Reasons to show that £1,000 from
Bristol is in good Proportion to the £40,000 of London," and
which contained these arguments, which must therefore be
taken with a large pinch of salt.

It is true that there was plenty of trouble during the
reigns of the first two Stuarts. There was good reason to raise
ship money for the suppression of pirates: for the *Matthew and
Sarah* of Bristol, among other English ships, was taken by
Turks and her master became a slave to the Emperor of
Morocco; corsairs entered the Severn; "Biscayners" and Dutch
capers sailed the Channel; Algerian pirates landed within
twelve miles of Bristol and took their captives into slavery;
and English vessels were captured and plundered even by
Englishmen. The wine trade also suffered from alternating
gluts and shortages, and both provided propaganda for the
advocates of beer. One poet wrote:

> Some that are scarce with forty pence a yeare,
> Will hardly make a meale with Ale or Beere:
> And will discourse, that wine doth make good blood,
> Concocts his meat, and make digestion good,
> . . . Thus Bacchus is ador'd and deifide
> And we Hispanializ'd and Frenchifide:

and another a few years later:

> Why should I deal with sharking Rookes, that
>   seeke poore gulls to cosen,
> To give twelve pence a quart for wine? of
>   ale t'will buy a dozen.

Yet if it was a time of confusion and danger, it was also a time of opportunity and adventure. Some Bristol merchants were interested in ventures stretching from the North-west Passage and Newfoundland to the Barbary and Guinea coasts, Persia, India and the Far East; and meanwhile the port books recorded the arrival of large quantities of wine from France, Spain and the Canaries which neither pirates nor financial burdens on the trade could stop.

On Sack

Spanish wine was in great demand. We need go no further than Shakespeare to know the fame of sack in his day; though he confused its chronology by putting his noblest praises of it into the mouth of Sir John Falstaff, who lived and died long before the name of Sack, so far as we know, was ever heard or spoken. The very meaning of the word is as confused as many things in that age. Although it is supposed to originate from the French *sec*, there are plentiful references to "sweet" sacks—one of which, from the pen of the town clerk of Bristol, has been quoted already. Further, though it was generally applied to Spanish wines, we hear often of Canary Sack, and even of sacks from Portugal and Madeira.

Perhaps these were the result of attempts to profit by the popularity of the genuine Spanish article. Certainly Falstaff's most famous utterance on the subject refers explicitly to Sherris (Jerez) Sack, to which he attributes "a two fold operation": first, it enlivens the brain, the tongue and the wit; second it warms the blood, illuminates the face and fills the heart with courage.

The amounts consumed at a sitting were heroic. Not even Falstaff could do better than a certain bishop of Bristol who is recorded as having refreshed himself after a sermon with two quarts of sack. But the comparison is misleading. All wines as we know them are stronger than they were then; they have changed their character, as we shall see. This,

however, need not diminish our admiration for the good
bishop: two quarts of anything, even after the most eloquent
sermon, would be more than enough for any modern preacher.

1603–25   King James I, the first English Stuart King, was partial to
claret like many Scots, and had his agent buying for him at
Bordeaux: yet he bowed, though with an ill grace, to the
newer fashion which prevailed at the court, and ordained
"that there be allowed to the sargeant of our seller, twelve
gallons of Sacke a day, and no more".

Puritans and Pilferers

In the Civil War Bristol, true to its character, did its best to
remain neutral. But its strategic position was against it. It
suffered sieges, changed hands twice, and saw many of its
houses destroyed and some of its citizens taken to the
scaffold. The victorious Parliament men destroyed the
historic castle. But their Puritan principles did not extend to
a disapproval of wine. They encouraged the trade, which
began to recover from the ill effects of the Civil War; and
they set up a committee to "bring in a report to the House for
preventing the evil now growing by the great price which is
put upon Spanish wines". Yet they could not expect friendship from the Roman Catholic countries. Bristol merchants'
property in Portugal and the Madeiras was forfeit because
of their "good affection to the Parliament of England". The
Jonathan of Bristol, having laden twelve pipes of wine at
Fayal, was seized by order of the King of Portugal in 1650
and her crew imprisoned; and though they were afterwards
released it appears that they did not see their ship again.

Then Parliament embarked on another war against Spain,
with the usual results for trade in general. Thomas Shewell
of Bristol, asking for a warship to convoy home the *Samaritan*
and her cargo of wine, said that she dared not leave Bordeaux
without protection.

A less serious risk, but one which probably worried merchants quite as much, is shown in evidence given by Thomas
Hackwell, mariner, "upon his corporall othe voluntarily taken
upon the holy Evangelists of God". He had served on the
Tigre of Amsterdam, bound from Malaga to Bristol with wine
and fruit, and stated that it was the "usuall and constante
practise" of the carpenter gunner and one Jacob "to drinke

and tipple of the said wynes all day long, and most nights likewise". He gave the opinion that if the merchant had protested he might have been in danger of his life, for when he checked one of the seamen for being drunk the man immediately struck him. Perhaps, however, Master Hackwell was prejudiced. He seems to have been nursing some private grievance. His evidence goes on for several pages and his final shot is the statement (presumably connected with the prevalence of rats) that "there was but one Catt aboard during all the voyage".

New Patterns of Trade

With the Puritan dictator gone and another Stuart on the throne, England was full of optimism and extravagance. Charles II brought from France a new taste—champagne; 1660-85 and this was firmly planted in the fashionable world of London by his protégé, the gourmet St. Evremond, whom he honoured with the appointment of "Governor of the Duck Islands" (the islands in the lake in St. James's Park) at a salary of £300 a year.

Charles was short of money like his father and grandfather, and his troubles were increased by the Plague, the Fire of London and various wars. The maximum price in London for Gascon wines, which had been between 6d. and 10d. per gallon in the fifteenth century, was now fixed at 8d. per quart; Rhenish had risen in the same period from about 1s. 5d. per gallon to 1s. per quart. Then, to help fill the King's empty purse, Parliament squeezed the vintners for a subsidy of £310,000. The natural result was a severe depression. From Bristol came a report that "trade is dull, and that in wines quite knocked on the head"; and there was no sherry to be had there.

Once more the wine trade showed its vitality. It paid off that subsidy within two years and met another yet more stringent demand which followed. Meanwhile Bristol was becoming steadily more prosperous: it was stated in 1687 that the annual customs taken at the port on wine, oil and fruit from the Peninsula and Italy amounted to £40,000.

Now the main centre of Bristol's overseas interests was moving westward. Many of its manufactures went to the planters who were building their homesteads and their fortunes in the West Indies. They sent home in return their sugar, rum, indigo, cotton and tobacco. Sugar, which had come from Portugal more than two centuries before as a scarce luxury, was now becoming one of Bristol's staple imports and the basis of a new local industry—sugar refining. It was a favourite sight of the town to watch the white sugar-loaves made, while partaking of eggs fried in the furnaces and Spanish wine.

This prosperous western trade had its dark side. The plantations' hunger for labour was not satisfied by the swarms of indentured servants who embarked on every ship to try their fortunes in the fabulous new land. Many unfortunates were sucked in against their will to help fill the vacuum—some convicted criminals, and some whose only offence was to have supported the wrong political party. There was a crop of royalists after Worcester, and of Monmouth's supporters after the rebellion of 1685. Even kidnapping helped to swell the supply. Almost everyone in the city was involved in one way or another in this traffic. When Judge Jeffreys came to Bristol in 1685 he found "all the aldermen and justices concerned, more or less, and the mayor himself as bad as any". The mayor had a disagreeable time: he has hauled from the bench to stand in all his robes like a criminal at the bar while the judge addressed him as a "kidnapping knave".

But worse was to come. In 1698 the African trade, hitherto legally reserved to members of the Royal African Company, was thrown open. By the end of the century Bristol ships were shaping their course to a new pattern—one which revived the oldest and blackest chapter in the town's history. They started on a familiar route down the Atlantic coast, but passed their wonted destinations of Bordeaux and Lisbon, skirting the great bulge of Africa as far as the Guinea coast—then known by a more sinister name, the Slave Coast. Thence, having exchanged their cargoes of manufactured goods for human beings, they pushed out across the open sea. Their next call was at some port in the West Indies where the slaves—such as had survived the voyage—fetched excellent prices. In 1713 the mayor of Bristol said that the slave trade was one of "the greatest supports of our people".

The port towards the end of the seventeenth century

5   A vintage scene in Jerez. The casks are being transported from
the vineyards to the *bodegas*

6   A *bodega* in Jerez, showing one of the Bristol Cream *soleras*

7 Grapes being picked in the Douro Valley above Oporto

presented a lively scene. The diarist Evelyn compared it
with London, not in extent but in its bustle and business and
in the old bridge that carried houses above the river. Samuel
Pepys wrote a delightful account of his short visit, when he
saw a great ship building, and carts drawn by dogs for the
safety of the vaults and their rich contents, and was entertained by Mr. Butt, uncle of Deb, his wife's pretty maid, with
strawberries, venison pasty, and "plenty of brave wine, above
all Bristol Milk".

Bristol Milk, the city's particular sherry, was already
famous. Fuller described it in his *History of the Worthies of
England*:

> Though as many Elephants are fed as Cows grased within
> the walls of this City, yet great plenty of this Metaphorical
> Milk, whereby Xeres or Sherry-Sack is intended. Some will
> have it called Milk because . . . such Wine is the first moisture,
> given Infants in this City. It is also the entertainment of course,
> which the courteous Bristolians present to all Strangers, when
> first visiting their City.

The earliest use of the name which has come to light is
dated August, 1634. It is in a manuscript in the British
Museum, a record of one of those tours of the country so
popular at that time:

> "And so, with a cup of Bristow milk, we parted with our
> honest and grave host, and bade this sweet city adieu." The
> citizens seem to have attributed some great virtue to it, for
> in 1643, when Colonel Fiennes was on trial for his failure to
> hold the city against Prince Rupert, it was stated in evidence
> against him that "the Bristol garrison might have held out,
> especially being furnished with good store of Bristol Milk. . . ."

Gifts of the famous Bristol sherry were made not only to
private guests as Fuller said, but also publicly to those who
had earned the city's gratitude. Among these was its Member
of Parliament who retired in 1713 and received from the
Corporation one gross of sherry valued at £16 18s. 6d. A
modest recompense, for this was Edward Colston, a more
famous benefactor of Bristol even than Canynges or John
Whitson. He too was a son of Bristol, though most of his
business was based on London. He made his fortune by
trading with Africa, Spain and the West Indies, and his

public charities are said to have totalled over £70,000. The city still celebrates his birthday every year and has given his name to one of its chief streets and to its great concert hall. But his finest memorial is the school which he founded so that boys might be "educated in the fear of God and the profession of His true religion as it is set forth by the Established Church of England". So when the great West Indiamen were seen no more, and the last sugar refinery was closed, Bristol had good reminders of that trade and the wealth which it had brought.

The Retail Trade

Throughout the seventeenth century the retail trade lacked proper control. Under the first two Stuarts the power to grant licences was "farmed"; that is, it was sold to the highest bidder, who used it for his own profit. The Commonwealth laid hands on licensing and stopped the farm, but only to suppress those taverns which were centres of Royalist propaganda: and after the Restoration it became again a royal privilege.

There was no hope of improvement until licensing was controlled for the benefit of the customer, not for political advantage or personal gain. An early attempt to achieve this was made in Bristol; and, as might be expected, it was made by the trade. In 1606 the Guild of Innholders, anxious that visitors should be "honestly, decently and lawfully used", asked for an ordinance. This was duly passed and contained twenty-one very practical clauses. Attached was a list of eighteen inns "fitt to be used": the rest were to be suppressed except the "Victualling and Tippling houses" on the Quay and the Back. The Company was to elect a Master and two wardens annually. The wardens were to search the inns once a quarter, check all measures and bring defective ones before the mayor to be defaced. Finally, any innholder "permitting incontinencye" in his house was to pay 40s. fine.

Unfortunately there were powerful persons who behaved as if the ordinance did not exist. It did not prevent Charles I from granting to Robert Wright of Bristol and his sons, Erasmus and Thomas, for their lives, licence to keep a tavern or wine cellar in their house in the city. Later the farm was sold to Lord Goring, who granted vast numbers of licences.

The City Corporation entered the field and obtained for itself the right to grant six wine licences: it paid the State £13 6s. 8d. a year for each, and disposed of them at £20, making a clear profit of £40 a year. Then the Merchant Venturers tried to get the licences for the city and its neighbourhood away from the vintners and into their own hands; but the vintners defeated them.

In 1700 Bristol had 240 inns, taverns and alehouses— roughly one for every twenty families. Two years later a limit of 220 was fixed, but by 1712 the number had grown again to 253.

Yet the better type of inn—and this includes many that were small, modest and rural—was good and clean, and remained the chief public meeting place. "The world affords not such inns as England hath", wrote Fynes Morison in 1617. The Puritans unintentionally added to their good cheer; for many of the musical instruments which they banished from the churches found their way into the taverns. The squire would go to the village inn to drink and consulted the landlord before choosing his wine. And if mine host was sometimes in league with highwaymen, he was more often an honest man, and at best a philosopher with unrivalled opportunities for observing human nature.

Politics Again

The effects of politics on the wine trade make an endless and on the whole depressing story, with the one cheerful feature that the trade always seems to have survived somehow. When the tide of Protestant feeling put William of Orange on the throne of England and another war with 1689–1702 France began, the duty on French wines was raised until it seemed prohibitive. Anti-French sentiments became fashionable; the papers took up the propaganda; the *Spectator* in 1711 condemned "this plaguey French claret" and praised "good solid edifying port". Yet the nobility remained faithful to their old love, and Bordeaux still sent them of its best. Smugglers grew fat on high duties: in the reign of Anne it was 1702–14 written that, thanks to the smugglers from Land's End to the Downs, the best claret could be bought for 3s. or 4s. a gallon although the bare duty was 3s. per quart. French wines came also via Spain and Portugal, mysteriously changing their

nationality *en route* so as to qualify for the lower duties; and
no doubt it was due to Bristol's special connection with the
Peninsula that in the eighteenth century certain French
wines were given the humorous alias of "Bristol Ports".

Other wickednesses too were encouraged by scarcity and
high price. Innkeepers were tempted to dilute good wines,
and to doctor sick ones with molasses, rice flour, "camphire"
and other less pleasant additives. A little book called *The
Art and Mystery of Vintners and Wine Coopers*, published in
London in 1682, purports to contain "Approved Directions
for the Conserving and Curing of all manner and sorts of
Wines". To keep wine sound and fresh, it says, "You must
fill your vessel once a month or six weeks with your best
Reeds you can get: for Reeds do preserve the Claret as Soot
doth Malmesey or Bastard." (It is a relief to find on a later
page that Soot is defined as "Wine boyled to a consumption".)
To help "Spanish-Wines that are sower", you must fill up the
cask "with 2 or 3 gallons of Water: after 3 or 4 days it must
be rack'd and filled up again with Rain-water; if the first doth
not do, some use Lome or Plastering". There is also a prescription for "making" Rhenish wine from a mixture of
"Rochel-wine", very strong scent, the whites of eggs, "Bay-
Salt or Conduit-water", honey and sugar, well beaten.

"Wine" was even manufactured from native ingredients.
The *Tatler* in 1709 referred to

> a certain fraternity of Chymical operators who work underground
> in holes, caverns and dark retirements . . . daily employed in
> the transmigration of liquors, and by the power of magical
> drugs and incantations, raise under the streets of London the
> choicest products of the hills and valleys of France. They can
> squeeze Bordeaux out of a sloe, and draw Champagne from an
> apple.

There were fresh competitors, too, among the new luxuries
that were reaching the country from east, south and west.
Coffee, chocolate and tea each arrived on a separate wave of
fashion. Each had its "houses" where people met, sipped and
gossiped as they had been wont to do in the taverns. "He's
no gentleman who drinks it not", a satirist wrote of coffee.
The appetite of the age was ready to try any new thing, and
to squeeze it for all it was worth.

At the other end of the scale were spirits. England had learned to make strong liquor from corn, and a native *aqua vitae* from wine lees. The government encouraged these home industries. In Bristol, during the war which followed William III's accession, the dearth of French brandy and the cheapness of Kingswood coal produced a crop of local distilleries. In 1713 a petition was sent from the city asking protection against French brandy and setting forth the great benefits of home manufacture, whose products were likewise termed "brandies", though their ingredients included cider and perry from local orchards, sugar and molasses from the West Indies. The sugar manufacturers supported the petition.

In general, England under the Stuarts had to cope with many new influences, new dangers and opportunities; and it laid the foundations of a new economics which in time brought greater prosperity. Commercial theories were worked out which brought huge wealth into English hands. Capital was being built up, and the financial methods which William III brought from Amsterdam helped the process along. These changes made it possible for England to become in time "the workshop of the world".

In the year before Queen Anne died another European war came to its end. England's power at sea was established: she had a firm footing in the New World and at Gibraltar, the gate of the Mediterranean, and the acknowledged right of trading slaves to the Indies. France and Spain could not now resist England's power, though their opportunity was to come. There followed a time of security for England; a time of German kings and contempt for France; of fox-hunting squires and comfortable churchmen; of coarse manners and cruel sports; of slow thinking and fast living; of Georgian houses and great gardens. This was the age of port.

CHAPTER IV

A Digression on Port

THE story of the Portugal trade is like the Aeneid; the gods took a hand in it, having destined great things. At the beginning of James I's reign, while Portugal was still involved as Spain's vassal in the dragging war with England, a covert trade persisted, especially with the western ports—chiefly in the produce of the Brazils but including some wine. When the new war under the Commonwealth ended, the wine trade began to flourish. The English merchants in Portugal were able to buy on good terms from the growers, who were neither so expert in their craft nor so well organized for business as those of France and Spain. In the 1690's England's imports of wine from Portugal exceeded those from France, the Rhine, and even Spain. But this was not the sort of wine we associate with Portugal today.

Large quantities of "Port" appear in London import records for 1682; but it is clear from other figures that little, if any, of this came from Oporto. What we know as port did not then exist. The wines produced by Portugal at that time, whether shipped from Lisbon or Oporto, were in fact beverage wines, though classified for customs, along with other southern wines, as "sweet". And, like all wines whether beverage or sweet, they were drunk young from the wood. This is the reason why no one before the eighteenth century ever seems to have mentioned a quantity less than one quart.

The first two years of Queen Anne's reign produced two events of great importance to the wine trade. The first was an Act intended to encourage home distilling and so to shut out French brandy. The second was the Methuen Treaty with Portugal, which included an enormous advantage in duty for Portuguese wines. This worked as slowly as the mills of God and produced effects which nobody foresaw.

The intention was to encourage imports of the light

beverage wines which Portugal then produced; it was hoped that they would replace French wines—which anything resembling port, at any price, could scarcely have been expected to do. The plan did not succeed; imports of Portuguese wine rose very slightly for a few years and then fell far below what they had been before.

Some Bristol city accounts tell the same story. In 1703— the date of the Methuen Treaty—the civic dignitaries, who for many years had confined themselves to sherry and claret, turned, not to port, but to Florence wine. Ten years later they had gone back to claret, plus smaller quantities of red Alicant, sherry, Canary and Rhenish. So far no mention of port.

On the other hand the Methuen Treaty did encourage the English merchants in Oporto, who persuaded the farmers of the Douro Valley to extend their vineyards. Production increased; but quality remained substantially the same. The gods still kept their designs to themselves.

The demand for Portuguese wines in England continued to fall off; and of what was imported the wines shipped from Lisbon fetched higher prices than those from Oporto. Still convinced that there was plenty of demand for their wines if they were good enough, the Oporto merchants formed an association to put matters right. Finding that the Douro grapes, because they contained a great deal of sugar, fermented too fast, they added brandy to check fermentation and leave some sweetness in the wine. This experiment was at first successful; Portuguese wine imports trebled between 1713 and 1728. But there was a reaction. These young wines fortified with brandy were neither one thing nor the other, neither beverage nor dessert wines. Demand fell off. The Oporto shippers quarrelled with the growers. The growers formed a company of their own. In 1757 there were riots in the Douro Valley and some who supported the English side were shot. The shippers petitioned Pitt against the Company. There was a long dispute. But the fact remained: these wines were not acceptable in England.

The solution worked itself out at length. The fortified Douro wine required time to mature. For this a bottle was necessary: not the old type of bottle, designed to carry wine from the cask to the table—bulbous and decorative, with a broad base for standing—but a straight-sided bottle which would not take up too much room during its long years in the bin; a bottle which would lie on its side, keeping the cork in contact with the wine, for a dry cork admits the destructive vinegar fungus.

Such a bottle was evolved; and in the next century, as we shall see, Bristol glass-makers played an important part in perfecting the method of manufacture. Add to this the cork stopper—not used in England for wine bottles before the eighteenth century—and the brilliant invention of the cork-screw: and thus port as we know it made its appearance in the world.

This was something to the taste of eighteenth-century England, already accustomed, since the arrival of spirits, to liquors stronger than claret from the wood. The imports of wine from Portugal exceeded 20,000 tuns a year before the end of the century, compared with about 1,300 tuns from France. Port took the place of sack on the table and in literature. It was now the national wine of England.

The new-shaped bottle, the cork and the long years in cellar were soon applied to the maturing of other wines. Wine ceased to be a "long" drink: it was sipped reverently from small glasses. To separate it from its sediment it was decanted; decanters and glasses became things of beauty. Colour and bouquet were added to the qualities which a connoisseur looked for in his wine. The eighteenth century was becoming refined, and wine was taking part in the change. A substantial home could scarcely be without its cellar; and the wine merchant became an expert. Locking up his capital underground perhaps for many years, he was bound to use all possible care and skill in his choice of invest-ment. His was a long-term business; reputation was every-thing, and he guarded it as his life. His customers, themselves perhaps about to invest large sums, came to him as a friend, expecting sound advice; and he made sure that they got what they looked for.

This story of the birth of port is part of the background of the age; it does not fit into a niche in the sequence of events.

8   Clos de Vougeot on the Côte d'Or, with the Château in the background

9   Treading the grapes in the *lagar* of a Douro vineyard

10 Broad Quay on the River Frome, Bristol

CHAPTER V

Three Georges

W E have remarked on the wine bills of the Bristol civic
authorities up to 1713. As if to mark a new era, their
first mention of port comes the following year, on the
accession of George I. Then there were no half measures. 1714–27
Fifty-three gallons of port was purchased at 5s. 4d. a gallon,
fifteen of sherry at 7s. 6d., fifteen of claret at 10s. (the prices
reflect the different duties), and some other red wines.

The fact is that "port" (at this stage, of course, the word
means no more than Portuguese red wine) was well-nigh
forced on the public by the difference in duties. Those who
had to consider their pockets could hardly afford to drink any
other. Had this not been so, no doubt the faithful band of
claret supporters would have been larger. As it was, these
were mostly aristocrats and rich men. We have two sets of
accounts for about the same period, 1720 to 1740, which
clearly show the difference. The barber-surgeons spent £948
on port, a fifth as much on Spanish wines, and £2 8s. 0d. on
claret; while John Hervey, first Earl of Bristol, spent some
£242 on claret, £30 on champagne and burgundy, and £65
on port.

"Sack" appears in both these sets of accounts, and in the
literature of the early part of the century, and then almost
disappears: but it was the name that went out of favour, for
sherry remained popular. The fame of Bristol sherry spread:
it was synonymous with Bristol hospitality. One important
person—Sir Robert Eyre, the Recorder—who had done the
city a service was voted fifty guineas for a pair of coach horses;
but he, preferring "your excellent Sherry", received sixty
dozen. Daniel Defoe was among the many advocates of Bristol
Milk, which he described as "Spanish Sherry, nowhere so
good as here".

Defoe had included Bristol in his *Tour through the Whole*

Island, published in 1726. His sharp eyes missed very little. He noted the merchants' widespread activities both on the seas and inland; and the encroachments of their Liverpool rivals did not escape him. Because all who were not freemen were excluded from trade, he wrote, the city did not spread, but grew by crowding itself more and more closely within its boundaries.

Alexander Pope described Bristol a few years after Defoe. Being a poet, he observed less fact and more scenery—the old bridge with houses on its back like London Bridge; the swarming crowds of seamen, women and children, laden horses and asses, and sledges piled with goods,

> without posts to separate them; and in the middle of the street, as far as you can see, hundreds of ships, their masts as thick as they can stand by one another, which is the oddest and most surprising sight imaginable.

It was a thriving, boisterous, romantic, squalid place, the Bristol of the early eighteenth century. The rich had their fine houses and choice wines. For the poor there was plenty of beer and cheap gin. The number of ale houses permitted in 1736 (excluding wine shops, inns and coffee houses) amounted to one for every sixteen private dwellings in the city; and eighteen years later the proportion was one to ten. The issue of retail licences was generally run for the profit of the licenser. This advertisement, which appeared in a Bristol paper in 1747, speaks for itself:

> To be lett by Alderman Nath. Day, the
> Royal Anne, at Wapping. N.B. There will
> be no other public-house admitted at
> Wapping.

(The place referred to is in Bristol; this was not the London Wapping.)

For those who made their excesses too public there were the stocks. Thieves of either sex were whipped through the streets; and the ducking-stool stood on the weir for the treatment of scolding women by the mayor's order. Bull-baiting, cock-fighting and "squailing" were popular amusements. The victim of this last was a cock, which was either tethered to a stake or tied to a man's back, and pelted or beaten to death.

This sport was part of the Shrovetide ritual, and was apparently a pious act of retribution on the bird for its part in St. Peter's denial of his Master. The theatre (we are still speaking of the early part of the century) was officially frowned on as immoral; it could only function outside the magistrates' jurisdiction, at Jacob's Wells. Sunday observance was strictly enforced with "a great face of seriousness in religion"; and prayers were offered for divine protection of the slavers.

Alongside all this, the great tradition of Canynges and Colston persisted—not only in noble relics and bequests, but in the lives of countless citizens great and small; warm-hearted charity; strong sense of duty; close cohesion of social and family life. Such contrasts are part of the age. In Bristol they reached extremes; for Bristol was, and is, a city of contrasts.

Bristol's main interests overseas were now firmly fixed in the new world—the American colonies and the West Indies. So, when there was war with Spain in 1739 and with France a few years later, old friendships caused fewer misgivings than before. Privateer fleets set out down the Avon to attack French and Spaniards with equal zest. Of these, the *Blandford* and her commander, Stonehouse, won such fame for their daring and the noble prizes they brought home that an ode was written in their honour; a work remarkable for its spirit if not for its rhyme:

Ye seamen who've a mind to go in pursuit of new adventures,
Repair on board the *Blandford*, with Captain Stonehouse enter,
Who cruising goes to meet his foes, such pastime sure must
    please us,
We'll prizes make of all we take; this will to fortune raise us.
Here is our chief encouragement, our ship belongs to Bristol,
Poor Londoners when coming home, they surely will be press'd
    all:
We've no such fear when home we steer with prizes under
    convoy,
We'll frolick round all Bristol town, sweet liberty we enjoy. . . .

and so on.

Stonehouse's richest prize—the *St. Phillip*, valued at £30,000—was also his last. His leg was shattered in the fight and he died after reaching port. The *Blandford*'s owners supported his pall as a last tribute to his courage and the wealth he had brought them.

Tough and fearless the mariners of that age must have been. The Bristol ship *Phoenix*, Captain Carbry, homeward bound from Malaga, was seized by an Algerian man-of-war and put about for Algiers under a prize crew. The pirates had reckoned without Captain Carbry. He fought one of them, who was armed with a knife, and threw him overboard, despatched another with the bar of the ship's kettle, regained control of his ship and sailed her safely to Kingroad with a crew of four men, one of whom had been stabbed in the scuffle, and a boy; and there he delivered up the four surviving Algerines in irons.

An Age of Change

But the time when toughness and self-confidence were sufficient equipment with which to face the world was passing; the seeds of a new age were sown before 1750. A list of those who were young men or boys in that year would include James Brindley, the builder of canals, John Smeaton and all the great first generation of civil engineers who revolutionized England's transport system; James Watt, Richard Arkwright and other inventors of machines; John Wilkinson, the iron-master; Josiah Wedgwood, the potter-industrialist; and Tom Paine, author of *The Rights of Man* and *The Age of Reason*. "Turnip" Townshend had died twelve years before, having worked out ideas on farming which were going to increase enormously the productive power of the land. The birth rate and the death rate had been following nearly parallel courses.

> It was between 1740 and 1750 [writes Sir John Clapham] that the gap between the two curves began to widen—leading to that greatest known change in the course of population which makes the years about 1750 a watershed in economic and social history.

It seems that the gods were preparing in advance for vast changes to come—the Industrial Revolution and a new pattern of society. Men must adapt themselves, and hard riding and hard drinking would help them less than hard thinking.

Few people, however, worried themselves about such matters in the 1760's. England had defeated France and Spain and held triumphant rule from Canada to India. London society thronged the Vauxhall pleasure gardens, consuming champagne at 8s. a bottle. Once more it had been proved that an Englishman was worth a dozen Frenchmen. As for the colonists in America, they must toe the line. Their claim of "no taxation without representation" was absurd; and commerce was a gift of Providence for filling English coffers.

This is a sad page of history. The outcome—American Independence—may well have been a blessing in disguise; but that does not excuse the stupid conduct of affairs. It is some comfort that Bristol merchants were on the whole—and for good reasons—better informed on this issue than the King or the Government; they elected Cruger—an American born—and Edmund Burke as their Members of Parliament, and there were some among them who stoutly voiced the American point of view. We may be excused if we dwell for a moment on the story of one of these.

Richard Champion was a substantial potter and politician, rival of Josiah Wedgwood and friend of the eloquent Burke. Both before and during the war he was corresponding with Messrs. Willing and Morris of Philadelphia, the great American merchant house which itself was founded by a Bristol man. It is remarkable that he could openly express such sentiments without fearing arrest.

In the beginning, though he detested the actions of his own government, his chief concern was to urge moderation on the other side. "To prevent the ill effects of Vice and Villainy of Men in Power, the People must be resolute, but without Violence in the defence of their Violated rights." He sternly rebuked them for their conduct which, he said, had lost them many friends in England. America, though she had suffered injustice,

could have given an example of justice hercelfe [sic]. She should have levelled her Resentment upon Administration, who really oppressed her, and not upon the Commercial and Manufacturing part of the kingdom, who were always her best friends.

But, once friction turned to war, he left no doubt where his sympathies lay.

May God grant that the Authors of this War, whose tyrannical Behaviour have [*sic*] driven a brave People, jealous of their Rights, to the necessity of throwing off a Government, which had first deprived them of its Protection, meet with their just deserts!

The recipients of these letters were real friends; and they had, it seems, almost magical power. Champion wrote commending to their care, in case he should be captured, one of his captains, of the name of Pocock, who was bound for the West Indies and had missed his convoy. A postscript added to one of the letters shows that Pocock was in fact taken by the *Sturdy Beggar* of Maryland. He was treated as a passenger and taken to "Martinicio", being, as he himself testifies, "used on board the privateer with the Greatest Civility".

Such friendships, based on the mutual interests of commerce, did not prevail against the will of "Men in Power". The outcome of the war was a staggering blow, especially to Bristol merchants whose ties with the West were so strong. One of them, John Pretor Pinney—head of a flourishing business on the island of Nevis with its home headquarters in Bristol—predicted his country's ruin as Englishmen have done since time out of mind: "Alas! I am afraid her Sun is set, to rise no more."

Her sun had not set, however. The English learned their lesson. They took life seriously, turned their chief efforts elsewhere, and so became still richer. It was in the West Indies that Bristol found compensation for its loss of American trade. More goods from the factories went to the planters, and more sugar came home to feed the refineries—one of the finest industries in the city's history.

There was a ten-year interval of peace with France, and the French wine trade improved. Yet here is a small but ominous sign of something amiss: Bristol took a smaller share of the reviving French trade—though it handled far greater quantities of other wines—than Liverpool. This was partly owing, no doubt, to its wider connections: but perhaps there was another cause—complacency. The older port was showing less readiness to seize an opportunity than its young rival in the north. Its weaknesses—abnormal tidal range, and a long winding approach, not dredged as it is today—became more serious as the size of ships increased. The close corporation controlling the city's affairs failed to make the improvements that were needed, and exacted heavy port dues which drove trade away, so that in time even Bristol merchants found it cheaper to import and export through Liverpool. Bristol still had a long lead in 1750; thirty-five years later Liverpool was far ahead. That does not mean that Bristol's trade had begun to shrink. It was still growing fast: but Liverpool's was growing a great deal faster.

The balance of England's industrial power was shifting to the north where coal was more plentiful than at Kingswood. If sugar was feeding one industry in Bristol, cotton was feeding another in Lancashire, whose population was multiplied by four in the eighteenth century. Yorkshire manufacturers, quickest to adopt new inventions, were taking over the bulk of the woollen trade from the West Country, just as they took the worsted trade from East Anglia. Though the west kept its reputation for finest quality cloth, a slow drift of workers to the north was setting in. At the same time the whole country was in a state of trouble and stress, owing partly to the very speed of its growth, partly to the drain of the French war. The workers were breaking up the new machines; the Bristol mob rioted in 1793 in protest against the tolls on Bristol Bridge, and eleven people were killed; Habeas Corpus was suspended in 1794; and in 1797 there was mutiny at the Nore and Spithead. Yet England's world commerce was greater than ever and goods were pouring from the factories. Wealth and poverty grew like sisters side by side. The change in the very nature of wine was part of a great refinement of manners—among the rich, that is. Just before the end of the century, when wheat was over 106 shillings a quarter and people were lucky if they could afford to eat bread that contained only 50 per cent. of potato meal, a letter in *Felix Farley's Journal* pointed out that the well-to-do were powdering their hair with pure wheat starch.

Though such violent comparisons were usual, Bristol's conscience was waking up. The ducking-stool had long since gone out of use. The slave trade was being relinquished, though at great cost to those who had profited by it: in 1771 only 23 slave ships sailed from Bristol, 107 from Liverpool. A few even had the idea that the unlimited supply of home-manufactured liquors to the poor natives in the colonies was

not altogether desirable. Dr. Tucker, a great Bristol church-
man and Free Trader, wrote to Lord Townshend as early as
1752:

> As to ye Manufacture of Spirituous liquors, . . . we seem to
> think, that no Harm ensues from ye exportation of them to
> our Customers abroad. Where as in my humble Opinion,
> whatever is pernicious to our Customers, will in ye end be
> detrimental to Ourselves. . . .

So far it was easy to ignore the signs of change, and only
pessimists felt doubts about the future. Whatever was
happening in Liverpool, Bristol's trade was still increasing.
The West Indies, since the American colonies had been lost,
were acknowledged "the richest jewels in the English crown".
The sugar refineries flourished, and rum was in great demand.
Bristol supplied the planters in return with almost every
necessity of a pioneering life. One ship, the *Britannia*, cleared
for Barbadoes in March, 1773, carried bricks, pantiles, lead
shot, brushes, nails, wrought iron, paint, brass, tinware,
twine, grindstones, gunpowder, shoes, harness, "millenary",
white lead and port wine. Some carried Hotwell water in
special Bristol-made bottles.

Bristol might have too many eggs in one basket, but the
basket seemed a safe one: and in point of fact its imports
from other places—apart of course from the wines of Portugal
and Spain, France, Madeira and South Africa—were varied
enough if too small in quantity. Here, among the entries for
one day—17th February, 1778—are beef, pork, linen and
hides from Dublin; oil, anchovies, juniper berries and marble
from Leghorn; from Memel, along with a load of timber, stag
horns; from Barbadoes, sugar, green tea, a hogshead of
"pailarnum", six elephant's teeth and two sea horse ditto.
(Sea horses' teeth! The words conjure visions of a fairy neck-
lace. It is a pity that other records show the name was applied
to something huge and lumpish of the walrus kind.) Besides
the business of the port with its mile-long quay and throngs
of shipping, Bristol had its industries. Ship-building and
sugar of course; cooperage; brass-works producing wire and
"battery" for the Guinea trade; copper-smelting; iron-
foundries; lead-works producing huge quantities of small-
shot for America, Spain, Portugal and even the East Indies;

distilleries exporting liquor (in spite of Dr. Tucker) to Africa; soap; pottery; brewing; and on the banks of the Avon nearly opposite Hotwell House, "a curious mill for spinning cotton, upon the principle of Arkwright's, but greatly improved". Hotwells boasted its own industry. It was setting up to rival Bath in a small way, attracting the fashionable world by the promise, or on the pretext, of health (21). It had become a principal place of resort (to quote the guidebooks)

> on account of the very great reputation which its waters have acquired in the cure of Consumptions, Asthmas, Diabetes, and many other complaints; the romantic situation of those Wells, and wonderful passage of the river winding its course between the vast stupendous rocks of St. Vincent. . . .

So we come to the year 1796 and to the Bristol which William Perry saw as he stood on the quay considering the prospects of his new business. It was a Bristol which kept in many respects its ancient character; still a place of trade, still a place of contrast and paradox. The old town, although it had spread beyond its wall and over the low land where the Frome had once flowed, still crowded itself within narrow limits. Its gabled houses pushed their upper storeys sociably towards one another so that two people at the attic windows could touch hands across the street. By day, a meagre strip of sky gave light to the cobbled alleys: by night they were pitch dark, for the scanty lamps went out at eight o'clock. But at Perry's back, around College Green and the road to Hotwells, was another world, where fine tall houses—medieval, Tudor and Queen Anne—stood among fields and orchards, and bird-song replaced the cry of "gardey loo". At Hotwells itself of an evening there was a brilliant scene—silken dresses, hundreds of candles reflected in gilt mirrors, titters, tattle and the lilt of violins. At the Bush Tavern, headquarters of the New West Indian Society, planters, merchants, sugar refiners and marine insurance brokers assured each other of the merits of protection and the evils of free trade, and watched excitedly each year for the first sugar ship's arrival, ready, as their custom was, to celebrate in claret at her owner's expense.

PART II

TIME MOVES ON

CHÂTEAU LAFITE

CHAPTER VI

The Birth of a Business

THE house in Denmark Street where William Perry set up his headquarters—with cellars below and living quarters above in true medieval style—was already full of memories of the past. It was known as Gaunt's House: its stone doorway and great oak door were surviving parts of a much older house built for the master of the ancient Hospital of les Bonhommes, founded by the Gaunts, which stood where Harvey's office stands now (35). The cellars beneath it had belonged to a still earlier foundation—the monastery of St. Augustine, whose orchards once stretched down to the river and gave their name to modern Orchard Street. Here was a fitting place for the storage of wine, where casks and hogsheads might keep their precious secrets among the age-blackened groins.

Perry kept his resolve to concentrate on sherry and port for the start of his business. We know this by a stroke of good fortune. The old records, along with much else that was priceless, vanished in flames on that grim November night in 1940. But the oldest of all Perry's journals had before this passed through the hands of M. André Simon, whose notes on it were printed in *Wine and Food*. The firm's trade up to the end of the century, M. Simon records, was almost entirely in Peninsular wines. Red port and sherry were the mainstays. There were small quantities of other Spanish and Portuguese wines—Lisbon, Bucellas, Calcavella, Mountain, and Tent for blending; some Madeira—a good deal more costly than port—and one delivery of Vidonia, produce of the Canaries; very little claret, less hock, and no Burgundy or Italian wine.

There was also rum from the West Indies, French brandy, Hollands and gin, and various sundries. "British Brandy", it is good to see, appeared in only very small quantities. The firm did some shipping themselves, but bought most of their wines in Bristol or London. Like most wine merchants of earlier times, Perry had other strings to his bow. He dealt in leather; besides bull and horse hides and seal skins the journal had some mysterious entries relating to "bassells", "Cordovan legs" and "body legs". (This was a family connection. The city records link the name of Perry with leather during the eighteenth century, though William's father was a scrivener. A Nicholas Perry was admitted to the liberties of Bristol as a currier in 1720.) He also handled a number of "Old Gloucester" cheeses. Strangely, these all went to two customers at Caerphilly: in this respect Perry appears to have carried coals to Newcastle.

From 1801 onwards Perry's name appears often in the daily records of cargoes entering Bristol port: it seems that he was doing more shipping now than before. In that year alone he received large quantities of wine from Oporto, Aymonte and Guernsey (M. Simon remarked in his notes on the journal that sherry was mostly shipped via Guernsey at that time) besides an odd variety of other things—rum, sugar, cotton and tortoiseshell from the West Indies, and bags of feathers from Dublin. A few years later he took a junior partner, Thomas Urch, son of a baker who lived on St. Augustine's Back, and, like Perry himself, a freeman of the city.

The first surviving original document of the firm came to hand, by a fortunate chance, just before the manuscript of this book was completed, through the kindness of a friend in the trade now retired—Mr. Sydney Raine of Birmingham. It is an account by Perry & Urch to Thos. Rolph, Esqr., of Thornbury, Gloucestershire, for goods supplied during 1807 and 1808—to wit, eight gallons of cognac at 23s. and 24s. a gallon, and four gallons of Jamaica rum at 17s. The receipt shows that it was paid by George Rolph, Esqr., also of Thornbury. Mr. Raine writes that "Tom Rolph, having consumed the 12 gallons of your rum and brandy, emigrated to Ontario in 1809, with a large family of children and his servants", and settled in the Niagara district, leaving a power of attorney with his brother George. It is perhaps too much to hope that this fragment of history may come to the notice of his descendants.

Now it is time to pick up another thread of the story. One of Perry's competitors was a substantial merchant and shipowner named John Maxse. As far back as the late 1770's he and his partner, one Meyler, were importing wine from Bordeaux and Cadiz, though they also dealt in a great variety of other goods; their chief business was with the West Indies, especially of course sugar and rum. In the 'nineties John Maxse & Company had an office in Clare Street Hall and several ships of their own.

Maxse's claim to a place in this story rests on the fact that he employed two captains, both named Thomas Harvey—father and son. The father had come to Bristol from Hayle in Cornwall and the Cornish blood showed clearly in his son's appearance. They were Maxse's favourite captains and generally received the best commands the firm had to offer. Maxse and the Harveys were more determined than most in face of the present depression and the risks of Atlantic commerce. They took out letters of marque, which meant that a ship could be armed and might sail independently of the convoys. The following notice appeared in *Felix Farley's Journal*:

For *KINGSTON* and *MORANT*, *JAMAICA*

The

Ship HECTOR

THOMAS HARVEY, Commander,

Mounting 14 Carriage-Guns, with Men answerable;
Will sail early in October, a running Ship. For
Freight or Passage apply to the Captain; or

Sept. 15, 1797.   JOHN MAXSE.

There is in the possession of one of the older surviving members of the Harvey family an oil painting of two ships (1). One of these is the *Bristol* of 459 tons, commanded by Thomas Harvey the first, and the other the *Aeolus* of 278 tons, commanded by his son, and that they were among the finest vessels sailing from Bristol at that time. (The registers show that Thomas the first was in fact master of the *Bristol* from 1807 to 1819, and his son succeeded him: previously Thomas Harvey junior was master of the *Aeolus* from 1809 to 1811 and from 1813 to 1818.) The figures just discernible in the painting at the rail of each ship are said to represent the two captains. They are conversing—across some sixty yards

of rough sea on a blowy day—by megaphone: and this is
quite consistent with their character as handed down. They
were by all accounts as tough customers as other mariners
of their day. There is one story of Thomas Harvey the first
that, having sat for some time at table with a friend, he rang
the bell, pointed to a recumbent figure on the floor, and said:
"Kindly remove Mr. Prothero and bring me another bottle
of port." It is also related that, when naughty children all
over England were being threatened with "Boney", those in
Bristol were brought to obedience with the name of Captain
Harvey. The old man perished in an Atlantic hurricane
together with his wife and entire ship's company.

Thomas Harvey the second (11) also had plenty of experience of rough weather at sea. Among the heirlooms is a fine
silver watch bearing on its face, instead of figures, the twelve
letters of the name THOMAS HARVEY (12). It was a gift from
grateful passengers who owed their lives to his seamanship
during a storm. There are many tales about him, such as
most families preserve through the centuries, especially if
there is an ancestor whose life was touched by romance. One
of these relates that, while all the ships in Bristol harbour
were becalmed, he was about to attend a society ball at
Hotwells when he noticed a rising wind. He cut the ball and
set sail at once, reached the West Indies and was back again
before his rival captains, who had attended the ball and
missed their chance, were able to leave port.

The younger Thomas Harvey had married in 1783 and had
several children. His wife died, and in 1805 he married again,
this time a Bristol girl, Anne Urch, by whom he had another
family. Anne was a sister of Thomas Urch, William Perry's
junior partner.

The eldest son of this second marriage, John, had a horror
of the sea (13). Perhaps this was the natural outcome of the
tragedy of his grandparents: perhaps it began much earlier, in
that instinct of self-assertion which sometimes appears in the
sons of exceptional and forceful men, impelling them
resolutely to resist the call to follow in their fathers' footsteps,
and urging them instead to seek a line of their own. At all
events it was so strong that John could not be persuaded
even to go in his father's ship down to Avonmouth where the
river joins the Bristol Channel. Very likely, in those times, a

11   A miniature of Captain
Thomas Harvey, junior

2   The watch presented to
aptain   Thomas   Harvey,
nior,   by grateful passen-
ers aboard his ship *Aeolus*

13, 14   Portraits of John Harvey the first, Senior Partner from 1842 to 1878, and Mrs. John Harvey

strong-minded parent completely devoted to his own voca-
tion would have paid little heed to such a childish aversion;
but there was no blinking the fact that the prospects of
Bristol shipping were now diminishing sadly. These two
factors between them decided the course of John's life and the
future of his descendants until today. He went into business
under his uncle—his mother's brother, Thomas Urch.

Captain Harvey, like his father, followed the sea until his
death. Like many captains in those times he became a man
of substance. During the 1820's he was joint owner with
John and Philip Vaughan of two ships, the *Bristol* and the
Feliza. The *Bristol* he commanded himself. He died in 1827
and his shares passed to his widow who sold them. She died
in 1840.

William Perry was dead before John Harvey joined the
firm in 1822, at the age of sixteen, and "Uncle Urch" lived in
the old house in Denmark Street. The name had changed
too: it was Urch and Prichard, for there was a new junior
partner. What little is known of Prichard will be told on a
later page. Nor is there much evidence as to the firm's
activities during the Urch and Prichard era, though their
name appears fairly frequently in the Bristol bills of entry as
receiving consignments of wine—varieties unspecified—from
Bordeaux and Cadiz. These are no guide to the volume of their
business, for they probably still bought some of their wines
in England.

This was not an easy time for the trade in general. The
duty increase of 1795 had been followed by a succession of
others. The end of the Napoleonic wars brought hopes of
relief—which were disappointed as such hopes have been
before and since. Total consumption began to fall. The rich
and noble, though their taste was crude (the "Regent's
punch" consisted of various choice wines lumped together
with spirits, fruit juices and green tea), were not lacking in
drinking capacity. Three bottles a head at a dinner was
nothing unusual: and at George IV's coronation banquet
820 dozen were consumed. But the general public had to
consider their pockets. They had put up with the onerous
duties during the war, but now there was a reaction. The
Press began to agitate for reduction. For ten years there was
no response from the Exchequer.

Clouds over Bristol

Bristol, too, as a port, was now launched on a long decline. Apart from economic causes, it seems to have been beset by a spirit of self-satisfaction and stupid self-interest. The Dock Company was controlled by the old clique of merchants and councillors, whose guiding principle was immediate profit. The dues they imposed on wine were double those in force at Liverpool and three times those at Hull. The sugar kings pushed up prices until sugar for Bristol was bought in Liverpool; and indigo for the West of England cloth trade was also shipped through the northern port. As to inland transport, the city appointed the famous McAdam as its adviser on roads; but they did not get on and after nine years he left them in disgust.

Then, in the 1830's, there was a burst of activity on the part of a group of Bristol men, who, with Isambard Kingdom Brunel as their engineer, produced a crop of projects—new factories, engineering works and warehouses, the Great Western Railway from London to Bristol, the Clifton Suspension Bridge (22), and the *Great Western* herself, the wonderful steamship which became a legend. Most of these schemes petered out, though the railway was built. The *Great Western* and her huge successor, the *Great Britain*, proved that Bristol yards had not forgotten how to build fine ships; but they did not prevent Cunard and Liverpool from winning the American mail contract.

Meanwhile the tide turned against slavery. The Emancipation Bill was passed in 1833, and in the next few years England's imports both of sugar and rum from the British West Indies dropped by a half. The basket which contained two-thirds of Bristol's eggs was falling apart.

Bristol in fact was conservative. It defended protection to the last ditch, opposed the growing tide of free trade opinion, the Peel Government and the repeal of the Navigation Acts. The *Bristol Journal* in 1839 denounced the penny post—"this new plan of Whig reform will be a more serious evil to the country than even any one of their more flagrant jobs"—and in 1840 the new devices of adhesive stamps and envelopes for letters—"the contemptible cover or black patch which the Government have been asses enough to sanction". By 1850

Bristol had not adopted Greenwich time. It was living in the past. Its fortunes, still pinned to the West Indies, declined with the sugar plantations.

It has been said that the world owes much to two classes of persons—philanthropists and agitators. Bristol's philanthropists we know. Her agitators came to her aid at this dangerous juncture with genuine concern in their hearts and barbed pens in their hands. Showing great industry and remarkable command of language, they marshalled their facts and delivered powerful blows for the good of their beloved city.

She was suffering from "tardiness and lukewarmness", from excessive predominance of wealth, from "a cold and chilling blight, the natural attendant upon pride". Thus wrote "Cosmo" in the first of twelve letters published in 1822 (the year in which young John Harvey began his apprenticeship) in *Felix Farley's Journal*.

> The Principal Bodies, which now govern and direct the trade of the port of Bristol, are . . . by the very nature of their constitutions, incapable of, and inadequate to, the removal of the impediments, which retard the advancement of our commerce.

He proceeded to enumerate the impediments in detail. "Poison indeed do your high Port Charges prove upon any healthy and vigorous system of commerce." He noted that the rich merchants controlling these matters had so fixed their scale of charges—40s. on every ship over 60 tons burden—as to bear hard on the medium-sized coaster and easily on the West Indiaman of 600 tons whose voyages were long and infrequent; and that those commodities in which these rich merchants were chiefly interested—such as sugar, tobacco and wine—paid far lower rates than others. He mentioned also the invidious distinction between freeman and nonfreeman.

Nothing much was done. Rather over ten years later the *Bristol Mercury* published no less than thirty letters from "A Burgess" (J. B. Kington), who began by drawing a sad picture of "stagnation or serious diminution of trade". Merchants have moved to other towns; ships no longer line the quays; shopkeepers have fewer customers; manufacturers who once had fifty work-people now have fifteen; artisans draw

low wages; property values are down and only the poor rate
has gone up. He enumerates the causes of this state of affairs
in much the same way as "Cosmo", and with even more
uncompromising thoroughness. But the chief value of the
book in which these letters were republished lies in its
appendices, which contain a generous collection of figures.
There is a list of dock dues imposed on each vessel—anchorage, moorage, mastage, etc.; rates payable on goods, such as
wharfage, cranage, dock-rates, town-dues; besides storage
rates, quay warden's and water bailiff's fees, etc. etc.; a table
of rates on commodities from alabaster and alkanet root to
zebra wood; and comparative figures of the totals charged at
different ports on a long list of commodities. From this it
appears that in 1834 wine paid 5s. 7d. per pipe at Bristol,
4s. 10½d. at London, 3s. 1½d. at Liverpool, 1s. 10d. at Hull.

Bristol has cause to be grateful for such sons. They
expended a great deal of effort and eloquence for her good
with no thought of personal gain. No doubt they made themselves thoroughly unpopular. It must be admitted that
they had very little noticeable effect on her, at least for a
long time.

Let us add something here on the credit side, though it was
an achievement of Bristol's manufacturers, not of the port
authorities. The part played by the straight-sided bottle in
the development of wine has already been described. The
next step was to ensure uniformity of size and capacity.
This was achieved by a new method of manufacture. Moulded
bottles were first produced, and the moulding technique was
patented, during the early years of the nineteenth century, by
a Bristol glass-maker—the firm of Ricketts.

Education of a Wine Merchant

This was what was happening to Bristol port while young
John Harvey was serving his apprenticeship. But at this
time he was not very much concerned with economic trends:
he was busy learning his trade. And a fascinating life it must
have been for an imaginative boy, in the historic house that
was his uncle's home. He soon knew every corner of it from
the great front door to the dim recesses of the cellars, where
the shadows of sleeping casks moved faintly in the candle-
light, and filmy, feathery growths, drawing life from the

spirits exhaled by wine, hung gently waving from the arched vaults. The old cellarmen told him that if a piece of this gossamer, the colour of clotted blood, fell on your breast you would die, for certain, by murder.

He learned the practical details of the business—ordering, stocktaking, book-keeping; he learned, in time, the art of tasting—the concentration required of brain, eye and palate, and how to roll the wine over the tongue so that, while the tip judged the simple qualities, the delicate organs of the root could distinguish the finer points; the importance of colour; the meaning of flavour and bouquet. He learned to taste unhurriedly and in silence, and always to take notes. He learned of the growth of the grape, of soil and climate and different methods of wine-making, and all the influences, from vineyard to bottle, to which the living juice responds as if it were a conscious thing.

And then he discovered that all this knowledge was only a beginning, and that he must acquire that sixth sense without which no one can be a real judge of wine: that if he was to succeed in his trade the goods in which he dealt must be to him personalities, each with its character, its gifts and its demands.

John Harvey's youthful experience was not confined to Bristol. After a few years he moved to Kidderminster. Why there? Bristol, as we already know, had been supplying the West Midlands with wine for centuries past; the merchants and their wares used to travel by the Severn as far as Bewdley, just as, in times past, the iron workers of Staffordshire travelled in the reverse direction with their families to man the growing steel and tinplate industry of south Wales. There was probably a profitable exchange trade between the great port of the west and the thriving carpet town.

But the immediate cause of John's move was Uncle Thomas Urch's partner, Edward Prichard. Prichard is another of those minor characters who enter the story, impart a certain direction to the course of events which affects the whole lives of people not yet born, and then vanish. One's curiosity is aroused. One would like to know more about Prichard.

We do know at least from a local directory that there was a wine business at Swan Street, Kidderminster—the present premises—in 1820, owned by William Pritchard. (The name is spelt with a 't' as often as not, though never by the Prichards themselves.) William was probably Edward's father, for both their signatures appear, with that of John Harvey, on some private accounts of 1829 still preserved in the Kidderminster office: after that date only Edward's name and John Harvey's are mentioned. The Bristol bills of entry show that an Edward Pritchard (with the 't' again) received a butt of wine from Cadiz in December, 1818, in the same ship that brought a consignment for Perry & Urch. So it seems that the Prichards were operating in both places, and that in Bristol Edward was Thomas Urch's rival before he became his partner in 1820 or 1821.

By September, 1829, if not before, John Harvey was a partner in the Kidderminster business. There exists a letter of that date which gives the name as Prichard & Harvey. It accompanies an account for £21 19s. 6d., and reads:

> Sir: We beg again to hand you the above Account and to request the favor of an immediate settlement. The usual credit on this acct. has been so much exceeded that we trust you will not compel us to make any further application.
> We remain Sir,
> Your most obedt. Servts.
> Prichard & Harvey.

It is rather regrettable that this letter is addressed to *"The Revd.* J. G. L . . ." and has been returned to the senders marked "No one of this name at ——" (the town is illegible).

The Kidderminster building, with its fine old frontage of half-timbered brick, is as fitting a place for the business that is still carried on there as was the house in Denmark Street. Its cellars are even older than those in Bristol, for they contain masonry and part of a window which belonged to a tenth-century chapel, and the entrance—now bricked up—to an underground passage leading to the ancient abbey which stood where St. Mary's Church is now (15). John lived above the shop, within sound of the business proceeding below, with his family: he had married about the time of his move, and before he left Kidderminster again there were four children. His younger brother Charles (16) had taken his place beside "Uncle Urch" in Bristol.

By 1840 John and his family were back in Bristol, the firm

in Denmark Street was Urch, Prichard and Harvey, and
Charles had replaced John at Kidderminster. Rumour has it
that, in spite of the social attractions of Bristol, both brothers
preferred Kidderminster; they tossed up for it and Charles
won. This at least is the version of the story as it is told today
in the Kidderminster office of Charles Harvey & Company.

A year or two later "Uncle Urch" retired, and Edward
Prichard withdrew to Kidderminster, where he worked with
Charles Harvey until he died. John and his family now lived
in the Denmark Street house.

What was the extent of Bristol's trade during the time
when Charles Harvey was first in business there with Thomas
Urch? The outpourings of "Cosmo" and "A Burgess" leave
no doubt that it was shrinking: but more detailed evidence is
lacking, for in 1831 the mob, inspired partly by the rejection
of Lord John Russell's Reform Bill, partly by dissatisfaction
with the shortcomings of local government, and partly as
before by the Bristol Bridge tolls, sacked the Mansion House,
destroyed the Bridewell, the Old Gaol and the County
Prison, released the prisoners, and—what is more relevant to
our subject—set fire to the Custom House, which was a total
loss along with its records. It was the worst riot in Bristol's
history.

The English wine trade in general was now improving. The
duties were at length reduced, after some years of agitation,
in 1825, though they still bore far more heavily on French
wines than on others; and consumption began to increase.
The next few years saw a great expansion of London clubs—
White's built their new house in 1825; Crockford's opened in
1827 and the Athenaeum in 1830—which started a new habit
in English social life. Then as now they were good customers
of the wine merchants.

At last, in 1831, the duty on all wines was equalized, except
that South Africa had a fifty per cent. preference. The
devotees of claret showed, as before, a certain perverse
independence: during the next two years the consumption of
French wines actually dropped. Then it began to grow slowly
and steadily. This was partly owing to the rising vogue of
champagne, which became so popular that several firms
began to manufacture an imitation in England, as in earlier
days; this concoction, paying no duty, sold at 24s. the dozen.

There was a crop of new shippers who used the latest adver-
tizing methods to popularize their brands. The old-established
merchants and shippers, to protect themselves, drew closer
together. This was all to the good. The names of the great
champagne shippers—Perrier-Jouët, Clicquot, Heidsieck and
others—became well known. The merchants on their part
took a closer interest in the origins of their wines and began
to visit Rheims every year to taste and select as they visited
Bordeaux and Oporto.

Yet—such was the position to which French wines had
been reduced in England by discrimination—many more
years passed, and a further, more radical change was made in
the basis of customs duties, before the import of wines from
France began to compare in quantity with those from either
Spain or Portugal.

How John Harvey and his firm fared through the crisis of
the 'forties we do not know. At least he did not limit his
family, which reached a total of eight—four boys and four
girls. And soon he moved to the prosperous suburb of
Clifton, whose Regency crescents still retain their exterior
charm, looking out to the south across the smoke and business
of the city below, and westward over the steep descent
of St. Vincent's Rocks to the Avon Gorge and Leigh Woods
beyond.

The family were given just that kind of upbringing which
so many English children were receiving at that time. It is a
thing which no one who tries to understand British industry
and commerce as it is today can afford to ignore; you will
find its influence working right through the story of almost
every firm that can trace its origins back a hundred years.
Its essence was obedience and sense of duty. It was certainly stern. There is a story of one of the Harvey boys who
was being sent to school at the age of four, and asked his
mother: "Mama, what shall we have for dessert at school?"
She answered: "My dear, you will have books for dessert."
And if any of them brought home a prize, she would say:
"That, and better, will do."

Yet behind this sternness there was great love. The ties
that were woven were strong; and they reached out from the
family to the city and from the city to the nation. They were
the strength of Victorian England. They consisted not only

15 An ancient corner of the cellars in Charles Harvey and Company's premises at Kidderminster

16 Charles Harvey the first

17 A view of the Floating Dock, Bristol, in 1860, showing the tower of St. Stephen's Church, the Tontine warehouses and the drawbridge

of prohibitions and rules: there was immense vitality and enjoyment of life. In time the Harvey children's activities spread to business, church and municipal affairs, music, literature, sport and travel; and to everything they brought the same tremendous zest. Very few of them lived to a great age: perhaps they gave themselves too completely for that. But no one who has attempted to see that generation as they were can help admiring them—not only for their achievements, but also for their capacity of enjoyment.

Champagne and Speculation

The new half-century started in fine style. The Great Exhibition in its fantastic glass palace showed the world—and Britain—what British manufacturers could do. If their taste was non-existent they made up for it in invention and energy. Depression still lurked in the provinces; there was fear of riots in London marring the great occasion. No such thing happened, and perhaps relief added to the general spirit of buoyancy. (John Harvey was there, of course, with his children. The family still have some of the wine glasses, finely cut and engraved, which he bought there.) Gold—it was found in Australia as well as California—spread its heady promise across the sky. Speculation was widespread; and the lavish spending of the successful was more apparent than the stintings of those who had lost.

There was speculation in the wine trade also. New companies appeared and vanished. The reputations of old-established firms suffered with the rest. Then during the 1854–5 agony of Sevastopol taxes were high and morale was low. Consumption dropped. Only champagne continued its triumph: it was indispensable to the fortunate ones whose progress the bubbles rising through the golden liquid symbolized so well.

In 1860 Gladstone began a reform of wine duties. He first reduced the general rate, then applied a sliding scale according to alcoholic strength. The measurement of this property was, in the early days, a problem. There is a legend current in the trade that Her Majesty's Commissioners of Customs would assess each wine by taking a mouthful, spitting into a candle flame, and observing the volume of the resulting conflagration. If there is the slightest grain of truth in this it must apply to a much earlier date. Alcoholometry was already becoming a science, very largely due to the efforts of the Department of Customs and Excise. The commercial treaty with France which embodies Gladstone's new scale of duties expressly stipulates that strength shall be "verified by Sykes' Hydrometer". Sykes, and the inventors of earlier hydrometers as well, were Customs men.

To encourage consumption Gladstone allowed refreshment houses to retail wine, and introduced an off-licence for grocers. The results of all these changes were lower prices and increased trade. French wines, with their low alcohol content, had the best of the bargain: imports from France, which had been climbing slowly since 1834, more than doubled in a year, and thereafter continued to increase. In the London clubs good champagne could be had for 5s. a bottle.

The Franco-Prussian war put prices up again: "How are we to get on for Champagne if the Prussians are at Epernay?" wrote John Harvey the second to his brother in 1870. But imports from France showed only a very slight setback that year and then resumed their advance; and good vintages restored the balance of price. Total wine imports doubled in the fourteen years that followed Gladstone's reforms. That was a peak. The next thirty years showed some decline.

Slow Awakening

When Bristol Corporation took over the city docks in 1848 the church bells rang and *Felix Farley's Journal* predicted that "ere long Bristol will become the joyful mother of children who will make glad her waste places". The writer was wise in suggesting that his prophecy must wait a generation for fulfilment. In fact half a century was yet to pass in doubts, disputes and half-measures before the port was fully equipped to take its proper place in Britain's commerce again. What happened in 1851 should have been enough to show the truth. The *Demarara*, of 3,000 tons, newly built in Bristol, left Cumberland Basin under tow for the Clyde where her engines were to be fitted—and stuck fast in the Avon, blocking the passage. She was refloated and repaired at considerable cost; which would have been well worth while if the obvious lesson had been learned. It was all very well to propose improvements to the city docks; even if the citizens had

been prepared to foot the bill, the real obstacle remained—
an approach by seven miles of winding river, a continual
deterrent to big ships.

In the 'fifties Bristol was far behind Liverpool, Hull and
Southampton in the tonnage of shipping entered from foreign
ports; but more significant was the almost complete absence
of steamers. Bristol's Atlantic trade was still carried entirely
by sailing ships, a fact which the first issue of the *Western
Daily Press* described as "positively humiliating".

The answer was a new dock where the river joins the
Bristol Channel—at Avonmouth on one side or Portishead on
the other. But what of the cost? In any case these places
were outside the city boundary and such schemes should, in
the view of many prominent citizens, be left to private
initiative. But when a private company proposed to build a
dock at Avonmouth with rail connection to Bristol, it was
promptly opposed by the Corporation because its competition
would ruin the city docks. The company offered to compensate the Corporation for loss of trade, and at last agreement
was reached. In 1864 the bill was passed. The chief sensation
was relief to be quit of a controversy which, said the *Bristol
Times*, had been allowed "to break up old acquaintances, to
chill conviviality, to make men look pale and spiteful at one
another when it was introduced at table".

The first sod was cut at Avonmouth in 1868. This proved
to be the beginning of fresh troubles; but at least a step had
been taken. Meanwhile, in spite of all, Bristol port was in
fact progressing. Some improvements had been made in the
river channel and in the city docks. The tonnage entering
doubled between 1856 and 1870, which was a good deal more
than Liverpool could claim. Bristol was holding its share
of the trade in wine and sugar—a long way behind London
and Liverpool, but far ahead of any other port. The most
encouraging sign now was the wide distribution of its commerce. By far the greatest tonnage came from the United
States and Canada; the British and foreign West Indies and
South America were well represented; ships were coming in
every year from West Africa and the Mediterranean, from the
Peninsula, France, Scandinavia; and a surprisingly large
number from Russian ports in the Arctic, the Baltic and the
Black Sea. Bristol's eggs were no longer in one basket.

Meanwhile her agitators continued their thankless task with the same zeal as their predecessors a generation before. The pamphlet, *A Few Plain Words about Bristol*, written by "one who has scribbled at the desk", was a fearless attack on authority and prejudice—the "rampant spirit of party . . . a blind, obstinate spirit, now rabid, now dogged, but never inert, which has been peculiar to Bristol". It shows the same deep study, the same devastating command of English, the same humour; the same devotion to the city whose real greatness was itself a denunciation of present faults and failings.

Of the Harveys' business at this time there is no record, and but little of their family life. One of John's granddaughters went through a hoard of papers before they were destroyed. She writes:

> From an old diary we found that they constantly had family dinner parties of twelve or more—various relations coming to stay with several of their children, and married sons with their children coming to meet them. More formal parties too, and a ball at the Clifton Down Hotel.

He played the flute (John Harvey the fifth has that instrument now. It is dated 1826; perhaps a twentieth birthday present), one of his sons played the violin and another the 'cello. All sang in parts, and musical evenings were part of family life in Clifton Park.

Three young Harveys went into the business. The eldest son was named John as always henceforth (23). The second was Edward (24). The third, christened Charles after his uncle at Kidderminster, left after a short time. The two eldest were soon confirmed travellers on the Continent. John the second, in the letter already quoted, shows his familiarity with the wine-growing districts, for after referring to the Prussians at Epernay he goes on: "It brings the horror of the carnage close home to one when it reaches the places one knows so well." Edward was at Chamonix as early as 1865, for his brother wrote to him there. "Business," he said, "continues very good." That is all the information we have of the extent of their trade at this time.

In 1871 the firm became John Harvey & Sons.

CHAPTER VII

An Age of Confidence

THE second Harvey generation took the reins of the business in a fortunate time—a time of belief in the Empire, in free trade, in the power of British manufactures to penetrate all markets on price and quality alone. In spite of temporary depressions and German competition Britain's overseas trade was increasing fast, and the volume of shipping that passed up and down the Avon grew in about the same proportion.

As a contrast with the general improvement, in 1890 a single ship from the West Indies docked in Bristol. Refined sugar was pouring into the country from Germany; and so free trade finished off what anti-slavery had begun—the extinction of one of Bristol's historic industries, sugar refining. Never again would visitors consume their eggs and Bristol Milk while they watched the white sugar-loaves made. The port had returned to its ancient diversity of interests none too soon.

In 1871 the iron screw-steamer *Arragon*, of 1,317 tons, sailed from Bristol for New York. Next year a new *Great Western* followed, and then a fleet of others. But these ships were too small and the company operating them wound itself up. Meanwhile the Bristol City line was founded. Its first ship, the *Bristol City*, left New York in December 1880 and vanished without trace. In the next ten years three more City ships went to the bottom, and a fourth was wrecked in collision near Pill, blocking the Avon once more. The pioneer *Arragon* was lost by stranding on Anticosti Island in the Gulf of St. Lawrence owing to a mirage, which pessimists thought symbolic. Yet these gallant efforts were pointing the way to greater things, which could not be realized until Bristol possessed a dock that was safely accessible to big modern ships.

How often it happens that the crucial effort, on which the whole issue depends though no one may realize its importance, is singled out by fate for the most ruthless opposition! The Avonmouth company was in desperate trouble. It needed more money, and applied to Bristol Corporation for help. Meanwhile another private company had been formed to promote a similar venture at Portishead, and this also asked Bristol for financial aid. The Corporation called for reports and sent inspectors to both sites. Just before their arrival at Avonmouth that old enemy of engineers—bad foundations—played its first card: the dock wall sank four and a half feet and bulged menacingly outwards.

There was a stormy debate in Bristol Council. One faction favoured Avonmouth, another Portishead; a third still supported the city docks exclusively, while many opposed any large expenditure. All the old confusion and bitterness revived. In the end £100,000 was subscribed to Portishead and all help to Avonmouth was refused.

In 1874 the *Kron Prinz*, from Germany, went aground near Horseshoe Point, and lay there on her side for three weeks, bleeding grain into the water, not far from Brunel's suspension bridge—a reminder of the *Demarara*, pointing the same moral. Four years later the *Gipsy*, outward bound with passengers and cargo, stuck in the river. She had to be blown up.

The Avonmouth company, having raised the money it needed from sources other than Bristol, went ahead with its building. One Sunday night 130 yards of wall collapsed and two big warehouses went with it: the thundering noise was heard for miles around. There were similar incidents at Portishead. But the engineers carried on. Avonmouth was opened in 1879 and Portishead two years later. Both were under private enterprise, though Bristol Corporation had a share in the latter. There followed a time of fierce competition. One party in the Corporation still advocated spending more money on the city docks so that they could compete on equal terms; meanwhile their charges were reduced and they ran at a loss.

At last, in 1884, Bristol Corporation took over both Avonmouth and Portishead—the only logical course. Now each dock could be developed for its proper purpose, and rivalry was replaced by co-operation. The required improvements were made all round, and new port offices were opened in Queen Square—hailed of course by loud protests over the expense, with particular reference to the Turkey carpet in the board room.

In the 'nineties another vexed question, which had troubled the city for over a hundred years, was settled. St. Augustine's drawbridge was replaced by a fixed bridge, and the Frome above it, which had formed part of the harbour, was covered over. Thus, with improvements to the adjacent streets and wharves, the city centre took substantially its present shape. The extension of the city boundary to include Avonmouth and Portishead, along with other districts which were already suburbs in all but name, increased the number of ratepayers who would share the bills for future improvements.

By the end of the century Bristol was a modern port. Its river-mouth docks were able to receive the largest ocean steamers, and the city docks were equipped to handle all goods that were carried in medium-sized vessels—which included, and still include, wine. Decision had taken the place of faction; and although lively disputes went on—for new schemes, and old schemes in a new guise, were argued continuously—there was now a basis on which solutions could be found and action taken. The pessimists who had opposed any large investment in the future of the port were soon to be confounded by events.

The increase in trade did not apply to wine. Britain's wine imports reached a peak in 1873 and then dropped off a little; they varied slightly, upwards and downwards, in the 'eighties and 'nineties, but the average did not noticeably change, and Bristol's share dropped a little further. This, however, does not prove anything as to the prosperity of Bristol wine merchants, who may have shipped through other ports, or purchased in England as William Perry did. France—thanks partly to Gladstone's reform of duties and partly to the popularity of champagne—became again Britain's chief supplier, though Spain and Portugal were never far behind. In the 'nineties Australia was a strong competitor for fourth place.

Retail wine prices towards the end of the nineteenth century were of course remarkably low by modern standards, but perhaps not generally as low as those quoted in a catalogue issued during the 'nineties by Stokes & Company, of 15, The Hard, Portsmouth, a firm which was later taken over by John Harvey & Sons. Their offer of clarets from 12*s.* a dozen and sherries from 13*s.* is the more impressive in view of the solemn warning against "Advertising Quacks, and spirited advertisers", and the statement that "fine old carefully matured Wine can never be sold at a low price".

A Correspondence

Of the Harveys' activities during the last thirty years of the century the chief evidence is in their letters, which were mostly written when either John the second or Edward was on the Continent. These two were good travellers. They knew their way about, and wherever they went they met old friends—growers and shippers whose names are known everywhere—who took them to their vineyards, *bodegas* and cellars, showed them the sights, and welcomed them as guests in their magnificent homes, and in return, on their visits to England, received the same liberal hospitality in Clifton. They saw, tasted and judged. As they carried out this programme year after year their skill matured. They were experts. And— perhaps because their trade demanded keen appreciation— they did not lose the eye for a view, the sense of incident.

It is tempting to quote these letters. Here they are, the actual words written so many years ago, with no thought of publication; a direct glimpse into other days. A comment, for instance, by John the second on a visiting preacher:

> He was very original, commenced his sermon by a very free translation of St. Paul to Titus on Servants "not answering again" viz. don't give a saucy answer to your mistress . . . he was too long, over an hour. . . .

But this is too far from our subject. The greater part of every letter is concerned with the business and with wines. John writes to Edward from Denmark Street in 1873:

> The B.M. seal arrived this morning after my telegram, and we are sending his Royal Highness and Lord Aylesford's. . . . I see Trower's sample of 1858 not decanted has fallen fairly. I think we had better secure 60 dozen of it if it looks well in the Bin.

18   Bristol from Rownham Ferry
From an engraving after a painting by W. H. Bartlett, 1842

19   The South End of Prince Street, 1825
From a water-colour by Thomas W. Rowbotham

20 Bristol in 18

Brandon Hill   *From a contemporary aquatint*

21   A view of the Avon at the Hot Wells

From an engraving after a drawing by Paul Sandby, 1778

22   Clifton Suspension Bridge and St. Vincent's Rocks

From a lithograph, c. 1864

Edward, writing to his father from Paris in 1875, describes in meticulous detail the wines he has been tasting at Epernay: one "light, elegant and forward but nose peculiar"; another "not so agreeable—to me it showed a *green* bouquet". Then, to conjure dreams in the mind of a lover of travel, the names of places:

> It has occurred to me that when you are at the Italian Lakes you may perhaps also go up the Rhine, then cross France to Bordeaux . . . bye the bye Beddoe asked me to tell you on no acct. to pass Arles without paying it a visit.

John was at home when he wrote this to Edward in 1875, but he travelled also. In the autumn of 1879 he took his wife to the Médoc: they saw Barton's cellars, watched the bottling in progress and ordered twenty-three dozen of the best, drove to Phélan Ségur—"one of the prettiest spots in St. Estephe"— and home via Chateau Pez to a *recherché* dinner, which included (with a number of other choice wines which are fully detailed in this letter) "a lovely bottle of Rauzan '47 to drink our 'jour de noces' in".

Theirs was an enviable calling. Who would not wish to visit such pleasant places, on such agreeable business, and always with the sanction of duty? It all seems so easy, mellow and comfortable. But in fact there is no doubt that, at home or abroad, they worked extremely hard. Energy was born in them, and sense of duty had been inculcated at an early age. Others might live easily in that leisured time: these Harveys earned all the fun they had.

The young men referred several times in their letters to their father's health. Then, in June, 1879, a heavy black border appeared on their writing paper. John Harvey the first was dead. His influence remained. The life of the younger generation continued to centre itself on the house in Clifton Park, and they all bowed to the matriarchal rule of their beloved mother.

Their uncle Charles was still at Kidderminster. The next February (1880) he wrote to Edward to give some advice on an executor's duties, and reflected:

> On this day A.D. 1840 I left Wells St. to take up my abode here, in company with your good mother and yourself. How

much has occurred since that time! The forty years now are as a dream.

Not long after, he also died. The town of his adoption loved and remembered him; his generosity had rivalled that of his brother. The simplicity of his character, and his deep affection for the family, shine through even the few fragments of his correspondence which remain. He had no sons; his business was carried on by a nephew—James Harvey, another grandson of Captain Thomas—and a nephew by marriage, Frederick Jotham.

John the second and Edward continued their travels from Bristol. It seems that almost all the time one of them was away while the other remained in charge at Denmark Street; and they kept each other fully posted with news of the family, trade and vintages. John's journeys were not all to the Continent: he was also strenuously extending the firm's list of customers. On one occasion he was in Dublin, visiting and lunching in regimental messes—the Dragoons, the R.H.A., the Coldstream—and sending home urgently for more samples. He was often in London, giving sage advice to the clubs and taking their orders, and in spare moments dropping into the Abbey to indulge his taste for music. Doors opened to him of their own accord; his numerous friends introduced him to others; he was sought for. His letters radiate confidence and success. He had supreme gifts as a salesman, while Edward seems to have worked most effectively as an administrator. No one can say which was the better judge of wine.

In 1882 occurs the first known reference to "the Cream", which was, and is, the choicest of all Harvey's sherries. The name originated when a lady visitor was being shown the cellars by Edward. John, who was there tasting sherries, asked her opinion of two blends. The first was the firm's Bristol Milk, and the second an even finer Oloroso. She was a good enough judge to appreciate quality. "If that is milk," she said, "then this is cream." And "Bristol Cream" it has been ever since.

It was about this time that that great wine amateur, Professor George Saintsbury, became a customer of Harvey's. In his celebrated "Notes on a Cellar-Book" he wrote:

If Claret is the queen of natural wines, Burgundy is the King. . . . I was during the keeping of this book, permitted by the kindness of my already mentioned friend, the late Mr. John Harvey, to be possessed of a small quantity of Romanée Conti '57. It was five and twenty years old when I bought it, and in absolute perfection; indeed, more than one good judge agreed with me that it was almost impossible to conceive anything more perfect in its kind.

He also paid tribute to Harvey's sherries:

My cellars (and even cupboards) have seldom for fifty years been without a certain "Margarita", from some vaults in "Bristol Citee", which were originally recommended to me by an actual Margaret, its name sake and fellow-citizen.

Port too was bought from the firm by the Professor.

Early in the year 1900 I bought from my Bristol friends some small parcels of the very best ports then available, including a '70 (a really magnificent wine), and both '72 and '73.

John the second reached the age of fifty in 1882, and it was natural that his thoughts should turn more and more to the next generation. He had four sons. The eldest was John as a matter of course—John George Russell Harvey; but to avoid confusion with his father he was known by his third name, and "Mr. Russell" he remained to the end of his life (25). He had entered the correspondence long before this, writing in 1865 to his uncle Ned on the Continent "instead of Papa as he is so busy". He was initiated into continental travel at an early age, probably while he was at Harrow, for there is a postcard—undated, and postmark illegible, but commencing "Dearest Mater"—from Château Langoa, where he had been making good use of his time:

We went into the chai & I saw them treading out the grapes. . . . After dinner last night we went down to a large room where all the employees feed and where they were all dancing. I had some really good partners, country girls who had been gathering the grapes all day. We danced waltz, polka & a sort of Sir Roger.

Eddy, the second son, was at Cambridge, but spent the long vacation of 1886 at Denmark Street, where he "set to work with a will & will very soon be most useful". The following spring he went to Bordeaux and Sauternes with his father.

"He tastes a little every day," John told Edward, "and has a capital palate."

From that time on John's letters contain—along with the usual reports on wines, appreciations, forecasts, the names of places, hotels and people, introductions to prospective clients (including Colonel Thomas Kingscote, Master of the Royal Cellars), corrections to the proofs of the new export list forwarded during a holiday, and careful notes on extensions and improvements to the Denmark Street cellars—more frequent allusions to these two boys and their progress, all with a distinct note of pride and thankfulness. The two youngest sons, Napier and Dick, went into the army.

Edward was still unmarried. But the omission was now repaired—to the astonishment of all his friends, for he was in his fiftieth year and was generally considered a confirmed bachelor. The following, dated 9th April, 1889, is carefully written on a half-sheet of notepaper and addressed to Edward A. Harvey Esq.:

> We, the undersigned, beg leave to offer you our hearty congratulations on your approaching marriage, and to ask the favour of your acceptance of a Lamp and Flower Stands. . . .

There are eight meticulous signatures—the office staff at Denmark Street.

One of the signatories, now a very old priest, has described to me as though it were yesterday the scene at Denmark Street on the evening before the wedding, with the men drawn up in a row in the warehouse, and the clerks awkward and fascinated beside their high stools, while Edward himself stood by the wine cupboard and spoke to them, urging them during his absence to respect the authority of Mr. Crook, the head clerk, and reminding them that work was the highest duty of everyone. Then they all drank his health in Perrier Jouët 1874. Among the wedding presents were twelve Hepplewhite chairs which were said to have crossed the Atlantic many times in Captain Thomas Harvey's cabin.

The honeymoon on the Continent, which was to have occupied three weeks, was cut short by the demands of business. But Edward was abroad again in the autumn; and his nephew Russell wrote to him, quite evidently keen to show his grasp of affairs. He gave details of the firm's accounts with famous London clubs, and a report on the excavations in the cellars. Two Americans had called—" 'noseing around' as they expressed it". One of them, Mr. Braun, who "made his pile out of butterine! & is doing Europe for the first time", placed an order (he "cleared the Grafenberg '76 and Yquem '61", John wrote to Edward the same day) and left his cheque for over 2,000 dollars: he also gave an introduction to a Chicago merchant "who buys the best he can get". John wrote to Chicago at once.

This was not the start of the firm's export trade, for their first overseas consignment had gone to Mombasa in 1884. Nor was it the actual beginning of the American connection, though it certainly provided a great opportunity for young Russell to show his mettle as ambassador to the United States. Five years later, when the firm had completed its first year as a limited company, John mentioned in his Chairman's report

the great depression in Australia and America where we have many friends. . . . The accounts from New York however lead us to expect an early revival and the many additional friends made by J. G. R. H. during his visit to the States last year (1893) will greatly strengthen our introduction to that great Market.

In spite of depression in distant markets the report records a continued increase of business. The past winter had been "one of the busiest in my remembrance".

In June, 1896, Russell—who had already spent two years with Deinhards, the famous German wine shippers, at Coblenz —was honeymooning on the Rhine. The couple were welcomed everywhere by friends; but he still found time to taste wines wherever he went and to send his verdicts home to his uncle Ned. Edward himself went abroad later that summer. John wrote him an account of arrangements he was making for further extensions to the cellars and the taking over of "the Protheroe warehouse and adjacent side of Orchard St.". John was by now apparently on friendly terms with Colonel Thomas Kingscote, Master of the Royal Cellars; he mentioned that "Tommy" had placed another order—115 dozen '91 Médoc—for the Queen.

The Queen's Jubilee gave him occasion for much activity and a great deal of pleasure and excitement. He went by appointment to Portsmouth to visit units of the Fleet which was preparing for the review. Back in London, he drove to the Park and waited patiently for "my first view in all my life of the Queen".

He thought she looked remarkably well and bright, and admired the splendid escort of Life Guards. Then came the procession, of which he wrote a long account—mixed with the usual business details—to Edward the very same evening.

I will only say now that the Queen looked 20 years younger than her recent photos—I am afraid to say what she wore as I never remember ladies dress but I think she wore light colour— but the scene was so dazzling I may be mistaken.

These old letters contain no dramatic events, no brilliant characters. But, as one turns them over, voices become audible and faces become visible. These people are so like ourselves—and so different. They have so few doubts. They work without reserve, perhaps because they know that their children will enjoy the fruits of their fathers' labours. Yet they have time to give proper attention to everything— business, pleasure, the writing of letters. They do not find it necessary to pretend to unusual feelings which they have not, nor to dissemble the perfectly ordinary feelings which they have; the strongest of which, without question, is for the family, closely followed by business and never clearly separated from it. They seem very content to be what they are.

Memories

We have arrived at a time that is within reach of living memory. John and Edward died long ago; John's sons, Russell and Eddy, followed them in due course; but there is a lady very much alive who was their younger sister Ella. She remembers driving down from Clifton to fetch her father from the office, and the great nail-studded door of the old house which a German bomb destroyed, and the cellar, its iron gate hung with fungus, and its low ceiling that has since been raised, and the winey smell, and the flickering candles held in metal rods, and the cobwebby substance which a child, lifted up by one of the cellarmen, could gather in handfuls and carry to the open air where it vanished like magic. When she was rather older Ella attended the luncheon which was given to the officers of the cruiser *Bristol*, when they sat in the crypt on cases full of champagne and octaves of sherry, and drank Bristol Cream that had travelled to New South Wales and back in a sailing ship.

An old cellarman, one of the four who waited on the guests, remembers the date of that party—September, 1896. He also remembers helping to bottle 50 hogsheads of claret for the old Queen's cellar. That would be well over 1,000 dozen; they reckoned 23 dozen to the hogshead, more or less. He bottled a pipe of 1900 port, laid down by Russell for his son "Mr. Jack", the present Chairman, who was born in that year.

The bottling was done by hand. First the hogshead was broached, and left to rest overnight, when a sample was drawn, and Mr. Edward came down in the evening about six o'clock in his straw hat (they all wore straw hats in the office) to taste it while Mrs. Edward waited in the carriage. Then the wine was drawn into bottles, and the cellarman would choose a cork, feeling the sizes with his fingers, soak it in wine, compress it and place it in the neck of the bottle along with the "needle"—a piece of wire which provided a way of escape for air as the cork was driven in with the "beater", a kind of mallet made of *lignum vitae*.

The "boot" was an institution since time immemorial. It was a bottle—deriving its name from the days when bottles were made of leather—into which the remnants or lees were drawn off. Its contents were considered the carrier's perquisite: and it is said that the drivers used to fight at the railway goods yard for the privilege of taking a load of empties to Harveys' and receiving a glass out of the boot.

The old priest who as a young clerk subscribed to Edward Harvey's wedding present had many stories to tell. They can all be safely dated within a few years, for he left the firm about the end of 1897. By that time he had saved out of his 30s. a week and £5 Christmas box—a comfortable income, he said, at that time—enough to enable him to prepare himself for ordination. He thought that while he was with them he must have been a trouble to his employers; for besides being

an Anglo-Catholic he was a Socialist and used to speak at
open-air Labour meetings on the Downs. The brothers, John
the second and Edward, were both staunch Tories and churchmen—one high, the other very low, "almost Puritan". But
they never spoke to him about it nor attempted to check his
activities outside the office. Perhaps they wondered whether
they were doing right in leaving him alone. "I cannot make
him out; it's a strange business," Edward said. They could
not know that something like sixty years later he would be
speaking with the warmest gratitude of their tolerance.

His profound respect and affection for them both were
evident. As he spoke, the old priest disappeared and one saw
the young clerk on his stool, and his two employers, not tall
but imposing, handsome and rather severe, with their
bushy eyebrows and classic, clear-cut features; their whiskers
—long at first, and later short to the face as fashion changed;
John's courtly presence, and Edward's face which somehow
suggested the poet, calm and benevolent as a rule, sometimes
suddenly contorted by thought. He had seen the funny side
too; and he laughed till he cried as he re-enacted little scenes
that took place in the Dickensian setting of the office. The
brothers, deeply attached as they were, liked nothing better
than an occasional solemn dig at each other. The firm had on
its list a cooking sherry called Spanish White at 18s. a dozen.
One day John came in as usual, with his springy step ("like a
dancing master's", my informant said), one hand behind the
tail of his cutaway morning coat. He sniffed at a row of
glasses on the cupboard top, sipped, and spat as all tasters
do. "The Cream, Edward?" Edward did not pause in his
work. "No, Spanish White." The clerks heard and dared not
raise their eyes. John left without a word.

He was known everywhere as one of the finest judges of
wine in England. So indeed was Edward. One of his nephews
—Dick, who was in the army but had some experience of the
business too—wrote of him: "I suppose he was one of the
greatest experts the trade has ever known." And Eddy said
many years later: "Uncle Edward taught me all I know of the
wine trade"—which was a very great deal, for Eddy too
became an authority in his generation. The fact that both
Dick and Eddy were John's sons makes their testimony to
Edward's knowledge the more impressive.

23 John Harvey the second,
Senior Partner from 1878 to
1893 and Chairman from
1893 to 1900

24 Edward Arthur Harvey,
Chairman from 1900 to 1910

25 John George Russell
Harvey,
Chairman from 1910 to 1919

HARVEYS & WHITE,

(SUCCESSORS TO URCH, PRICHARD, AND HARVEY)

DENMARK STREET, BRISTOL.

PORT.

	♯ Dozen.	♯ Pipe 115 Galls.
Old, from the wood	34/-	£80
Fine old „	42/-	£105
Superior „	44/-	£110
Ditto, very old		£120
Vintage 1861, finest		£105
Vintage 1863, finest		£96

Hhds. and Qr.-Casks at same rate.

OLD BOTTLED PORT	48/-	56/-	63/-	66/-
Ditto, older	72/-	78/-	84/-	88/-	96/-
Ditto, Pints	25 -	30/- ♯ dozen Pints.
Ditto, „ Vintage 1847	46/- ♯ dozen Pints.

SHERRY.

	♯ Dozen.	♯ Butt 108 Galls.
Old Pale	30/-	£66
„ Light Gold	34/-	£74
„ Pale, or Gold	38/-	£80
„ Ditto	42/-	£90
„ Pale, ... Gold, ... or Brown	46/-	£105
„ Superior	52/-	£118
„ Ditto	56/-	£130
„ Very superior	63/-	£142
Extra superior	68/-	£148
Ditto	80/-	£180
Ditto	84/- 105/- 126/-
East India	68/-	£148
Amontillado	56/-	£130
Ditto	72/-
Vino de Pasto	54/-	£124
Manzanilla	46/-
Rota Tent	42/-

Hogsheads and Quarter-Casks at same rate.

Madeira, very supr. old	92/-	♯ doz.	48/- ♯ doz. Pints.
Teneriffe, fine old	38/-	„	£74 ♯ Pipe 100 Galls.
Vidonia, fine old	38/-	„	£74 „ „
Marsala or Bronti	24/-	„	£44 „ 93 Galls.
Superior ditto	26/-	„	£48 „ „
Bucellas Hock	36/-	„	£80 „ 117 Galls.
Lisbon, rich, or dry	30/-	„	£70 „ „
Calcavella	36/-	„	£80 „ „
Roussillon	26/-	„	£56 „ 115 Galls.
Constantia	26/- ♯ dozen Pints.

Hogsheads and Quarter-Casks at same rate.

VOSLAUER.

Austrian Claret	24/- ♯ Doz.	£24 ♯ hhd. 48 Galls.

BURGUNDY.

	♯ Dozen.	♯ Doz. Pints.
Pouilly	26/-	14/-
Chablis	36/-	20/-
Beaujolais	21/-	12/-
Macon	21/-	12/-
Pommard ... 1863	36/-	20/-
Chambertin ... 1857	88/-
Richebourg ... 1859	82/-

MOSELLE.

	♯ Dozen.	♯ Doz. Pints.
Winningen ... 1862	30/-	17/-
Grünhausen ... 1862	44/-	24/-
Scharzberg ... 1862	54/-	29/-

SAUTERNE.

	♯ Dozen.	♯ Doz. Pints.
Good	36/-	20/-
Château Suduiraut, ... 1861	66/-
Château Yquem, ... 1861	126/-

BARSAC.

Superior	48/-	26/-
Château Coutet, ... 1858	96/-

PREIGNAC.

	42/-	23/-

HOCK.

	♯ Dozen.	♯ Doz. Pints.
Rhenish ... 1862	28/-	16/-
Erbach, ... 1862	36/-	20/-
Oestrich ... 1862	48/-	26/-
Geisenheim ... 1862	48/-	26/-
Hockheim, ... 1862	60/-	32/-
Johannesberg, ... 1857	70/-	37/-
Marcobrunn auslese, ... 1857	70/-	37/-
Steinberg Cabinet, ... 1857	92/-	48/-
Schloss Johannesberg, ... 1862	92/-	48/-
Rudesheimberg, auslese, ... 1862	126/-
Steinberg Cabinet, auslese, ... 1862	180/-
RED HOCK. Assmanshausen	66/-

CLARET.

	♯ Dozen.	♯ Dozen Pints.
Light	14/-	
Medoc	18/-	10/-
Ditto	21/-	
St. Estéphe, ... Vintage 1862	26/-	14/-
Pauillac, ... 1864	26/-	14/-
Superior St. Estéphe, ... 1862	32/-	18/-
Superior St. Julien ... 1862	36/-	
Superior St. Julien ... 1864	36/-	
Batailley ... 1862	48/-	(1864) 24/-
Château de Beychevelle, ... 1862	54/-	
Château Palmer, ... 1862	60/-	
Calon, ... 1861	63/-	
Montrose, ... 1862	65/-	
Château Lèoville, ... 1862	72/-	36/-
Château Lafite ... 1862	80/-	42/-
Château Latour ... 1862	80/-	
Château Margaux, ... 1862	80/-	
Château Hautbrion, ... 1858	92/-	
Château Larose, ... 1858	92/-	
Montrose, ... 1858		42/-
Château Lèoville, ... 1858		48/-

VINTAGE 1864.	♯ Dozen.	♯ Hhd. 23½ Dos.
Pauillac	26/-	£26	25/1
Superior St. Julien	36/-	£36	33/7
Batailley	44/-	£44	40/5
Pontet Canet	48/-	£48	43/10
Château de Beychevelle	54/-	£56	50/7
Château Langoa	60/-	£63	56/7
Château Lèoville-Barton		£72	64/3
Château Lèoville-Lascazes		£72	64/3
Château Lèoville-Poyféré		£72	64/3
Château Larose		£72	64/3
Château Lafite		£94	83/-
Château Latour		£94	83/-

Proportionate Cost ♯ Doz., Bottles included. Half/Hhds. at same rate.

CHAMPAGNE.

	♯ doz.	♯ 3 doz. Case.	For 9 dozen.
Sparkling	40/-	£5 14	36/-
Ditto, ... own brand	48/- nett		
Fine ditto	56/-	£8	51/-
Perrier Jouet, 1st quality sparkling	63/-	£9	57/-
Moët and Chandon, ditto	63/-	£9	57/-
Perrier Jouet, Finest quality, creaming, 1861	70/-	£10	64/-
Veuve Clicquot	72/-	£10 7	69/-
Louis Roederer's, Carte Blanche	72/-	£10 7	69/-
Pints ... 21/- 24/- nett	30/-	34/- 36/-	40/- ♯ doz. Pints.
Half-pints, finest quality, creaming	20/- ♯ doz. Half-pints.

SPARKLING MOSELLE.

	♯ doz.	♯ 3 doz. Case.	For 9 dos.
Sparkling, light	40/-	£5 14	36/-
Ditto, Muscatel	52/-	£7 10	48/-
Ditto, finest „	60/-	£8 10	55/-
Ditto, Nonpareil, ... 1862	60/-	£8 10	55/-
Ditto, Scharzberg, ... do.	60/-	£8 10	55/-
Pints ... 21/- 28/- 32/- ♯ doz. Pints.

SPARKLING HOCK.

Fine sparkling	52/-	£7 10	48/-
Finest, Ehrenbreitstein,	63/-	£9	57/-
Pints ... 28/- 34/- ♯ doz. Pints.

ST. PERAY, 1st quality

ST. PERAY, 1st quality	48/-	£6 15
Pints ... 26/- ♯ doz. Pints.

SPARKLING BURGUNDY.

	♯ doz.	♯ 3 doz. Case.
Red or White	56/-	£8

SPIRITS.

	♯ Gallon.	♯ 1 doz. Case.
Old Cognac Brandy, brown	24/- 30/-	
Old ditto, pale	24/- 30/- 34/- 48/-	60/- 72/-
Old Jamaica Rum	18/- 20/-	
Holland Geneva	18/-	36/-
Old Scotch Whisky	20/- 22/-	
Old Irish ditto	19/- 23/-	
London Gin	16/- 17/-	
Milk Punch	42/- per doz.	

FOREIGN LIQUEURS.

	♯ Bottle.	♯ Pint.
Curaçao	9/-	5/-
Maraschino	10/-	5/6
Noyau	10/-	5/6
Copenhagen Cherry Brandy	8/-	4/6
Grande Chartreuse (green)		7/-
Trappistine (green)		6/6
&c. &c.		

Six Months' Credit, or Five per Cent. Discount for prompt payment.

26   A Harvey wine list of 1867
(See Appendix, page 155)

Many odd recollections have been preserved by chance from these closing years of the last century. Some of the customers are remembered. There was one—over six feet and bulky, perfectly tailored in loud check, his beaming red clean-shaven face framed by long side-whiskers beneath a white Ascot hat. When the clerks heard a heavy step and a booming "Good morning, John" they would say: "Stewart's coming". He would enter with a cheerful word for all, and leave with a series of loud "Good days" all down the passage. The firm made a practice of sending its customers a Christmas gift—the best Portuguese dried fruit—and "Stewart" always came in next morning to thank them, with his loud "Good morning, John", and then "Good day" to all.

Then there was an old lady who kept a boarding house in Clifton. She came in regularly, in her black silk dress, bonnet, ringlets and lace shawl, to pay her bill—38s. for four quarts of Irish whiskey—and to place another order: it must be the same; she "didn't like the smoky". She was always received with the same consideration as if she had been a duchess.

But if one is remembered and another forgotten it is only a matter of chance. All were known and welcomed, and all contributed to the life of the little world of Denmark Street. The directors would speak to them as friends and advise them as friends. John never minced words; if a customer favoured an inferior sort he would say, "All right, if you don't want the pearls don't have the pearls." He could talk wine easily with the noble, the self-made and the humble—and take their orders. Edward, though he also travelled much on the Continent, spent more time in the office. The men and the clerks knew him as a driver, a stickler for detail; if anyone asked for half an hour off he would generally go deaf. But there was an underlying kindliness which ensured his authority. If any of the staff was sick or in trouble he was helped with gifts and, more, by personal interest; and Christmas was brightened by such delectable items as golden sovereigns and hams all round.

John and Edward, like their father, were generous to a fault; and, though they preferred their good deeds to be anonymous, there were many charitable causes and many individuals in the city who had reason to be grateful to them. John was the prime mover in the building of St. Mary's

Church in Leigh Woods—the district facing Clifton across the Avon Gorge and linked to it by the famous Suspension Bridge —where a number of prosperous citizens had already made their homes. He was also among the chief contributors of funds for the building. Some who were in the office at the time thought that he was over-liberal, and that this was a serious drain on his finances. Edward, whose Anglicanism was of a different shade, did not altogether approve—the brothers enjoyed the privilege of disapproving of each other on occasions—although his own benefactions elsewhere were equally generous.

Those who served at Denmark Street, above or below stairs, had reason to be content, and they responded with loyalty. At least two of the younger workmen at that time stayed with the firm more than fifty years. Henry Hodge became foreman and Albert Nelmes head cellarman. They are still remembered. Hodge, with his mutton-chop whiskers, had a dignity which bespoke his previous calling: he had been a butler for a short time. He was a hard taskmaster. He timed the men in at 7 a.m., and there was a seat, called the penitence form, outside the door on which anyone who was late had to sit until he had been reported to the Chairman. One unfortunate man, who was placed there on a snowy day and forgotten, was found hours later looking like a snowman: he had not dared to move. Hodge retired after sixty-five years' service, and when he died, although he had received no more than the good wages of two guineas a week plus free coal and light, he left £10,000. Edward Harvey had been in the habit of occasionally giving him small blocks of shares in Bristol firms, and these had appreciated in value.

Albert Nelmes, like his employers, was a singer and a member of his church choir. He ruled the cellars with his deep bass voice, and his exacting standards earned him the nickname of "Nabob" among the men.

The business was being built up on sound foundations. Harvey's had the Royal Warrant, and their name stood well with club secretaries and regimental mess presidents. The branch at Portsmouth was taking orders worth perhaps £500 from Her Majesty's ships, which normally sailed on a three-year commission, on the understanding that anything uncon-sumed at the end of the voyage would be returned for credit.

Eddy's sojourn at Cambridge had been the beginning of a substantial connection with the common rooms at both senior universities. The export trade spread east to India, China and Australia, south to the African colonies, west to Canada and the United States. In July, 1897, John wrote to Edward:

> It will be necessary to make important additions or changes in our Office Staff to prevent the Energy of the Partners being wasted. Trade is really good & opening in every direction.

He seems to have been thinking more and more of provision for the future. Perhaps it was due to a sense of his own advancing years, and the fact that he and his brother both suffered from heart trouble. A month earlier he had written with reference to the death of an old friend:

> These reminders at home & abroad & our own more frequent breakdowns are very plain warnings to ourselves & it is a great blessing to our families that we have successors & have been able to Establish an heirloom.

But he was still immersed in business. In 1899 he was criticizing the Chancellor's latest proposals for revised wine duties.

> I met Archdale Palmer who says Sir Michael's figures are incorrect—they are pressing him to tax British Wine which is so largely used for mixing. I shall give Lord Jersey a call in the morning and then see friends in the City.

That is his last surviving letter. He died in June 1900. The funeral service, at the church in Leigh Woods which he had helped to build, was attended by a great gathering—the family (but not Dick or Napier, his two younger sons: they were both in the army in South Africa); the Bishop and Archdeacon of Bristol; the High Sheriff, John Harvey's successor in that office; representatives of Clifton College, of the commercial and public life of Bristol, and of the various charities he had supported; and almost the whole staff of Denmark Street. In the city flags flew at half-mast, blinds were drawn and windows shuttered. John Harvey the second had served the firm for fifty-four years.

CHAPTER VIII

Sun and Shadow

FEW of us can remember what it feels like to cross the line that marks the end of a century. To some, no doubt, it means nothing. For others perhaps it gives a special solemnity to the retrospects, hopes and good resolutions that every New Year brings. Whatever its significance, the end of the nineteenth century was soon overshadowed by the passing 1837–1901 of another symbol. Queen Victoria's reign had been the longest in the history of the English crown; and throughout the Empire it stood for much more than length of years. Victorian prosperity continued for a time, and after the 1901–10 mourning was over the jovial personality of Edward VII shed a new cheerfulness on England. Life assumed—so it seems to us now—an Elysian freedom from care, an effervescence like champagne. The Edwardian age calls to our minds pictures of four-in-hands on the road to Ascot, the pearly glory of the costermonger, the rowdy hilarity of Hampstead Heath and the music hall.

The family was still the pivot of life. Fortunes still passed from father to son. Army officers, professional and business men could afford to live well, and large quantities of wine, especially port, were purchased for the cellar. In each of the five years up to 1910 Britain's imports of wine—slightly less in total than during the previous decade—included at least a million gallons of champagne.

Joseph Chamberlain's campaign for tariff reform was defeated and the Liberals entered on another ten years of 1905–15 rule. Peace and free trade were still the watchwords for England. But clouds began to gather over Europe. King Edward's detested nephew, the Kaiser, was rattling his sabre. Germany was building warships, and the British Navy took steps to keep ahead.

In Bristol the new century brought confirmation for the

optimists, rewards for past efforts, and occasions for further expansion. The Prince of Wales (this was before Queen Victoria's death) came down to cut the first sod for a great new dock at Avonmouth which was to bear his name. (It was he who on another occasion uttered the famous dictum on Bristol Milk: "All I can say is, you've got dam' fine cows.") A new Dock Committee took office in 1901, and a mission crossed the Atlantic to draw the attention of the western world to the merits of the modernized port of the west. By 1904 the shipping entering the docks, including Avonmouth and Portishead, from foreign ports exceeded a million tons, with a greatly increased proportion from the Americas: it was to be doubled again within twenty-one years. Bristol's total had been under a quarter of a million tons in 1860 and just past the half-million in 1880.

The Chicago Harbour Commission published in 1908 the results of a survey of important harbours throughout the world. Mr. J. Paul Goode's report on Bristol contained these words concerning the Royal Edward Dock at Avonmouth, then just completed: "Such construction is planned for a thousand years. There is no finer anywhere. It makes one hang his head for the shabby and shoddy stuff we line our rivers with." And in general:

> In all my tour of a score of the world's great ports I found nowhere more earnest zeal for the development of the port and the city than was in evidence in Bristol. The whole community moves as one man, and at a pace and with an earnestness and wisdom that must succeed.

Bristol's agitators were in their graves long since. It is to be hoped that they were allowed to know the longed-for change of spirit had come—and that, should the "blind, obstinate spirit which has been peculiar to Bristol" ever return, they will come back to whisper their harsh and salutary words in the ears of living journalists.

Bristol's historic trade routes were now as busy as they had ever been, though the cargoes were rarely the same. West Africa's staple product was no longer slaves but cocoa. The United States were shipping increased quantities of tobacco to fill the huge bonded warehouses, and petroleum— a comparative *parvenu* whose great days were yet to come.

Tobacco came also from Rhodesia and Nyasaland, timber and grain from Canada; from the Antipodes, frozen meat (for which modern cold storage was provided in the docks), butter, cheese, grain and zinc ore. Some of these imports were the raw materials for old-established local manufactures, now grown beyond recognition—Fry's chocolate, founded in 1728, and W. D. & H. O. Wills, of tobacco fame, some sixty years younger. Many other old Bristol industries—glass, pottery, paint, ship-building, rope and metal work—helped to swell the volume of imports or exports. There were new industries too: the Bristol Aeroplane Company was founded as long ago as 1910. With its coastwise shipping, roads, railways and canals, Bristol was handling exports of steel and tinplate from South Wales and the multifarious manufactures of the Midlands, and supplying these districts with imports in exchange.

The West Indies trade came back. In 1901 the mail contract was awarded to Bristol, and by 1910 twenty steamers of the Elders & Fyffes Line were plying between the islands and the port—bringing home, not sugar, but bananas. Wine imports remained fairly steady through the first fourteen years of the century.

New Hands on the Wheel

To John Harvey & Sons the year 1900 brought a new chairman—but no stranger, and as well versed in the mysteries of the trade as the one they had lost: his brother Edward (24). Thanks to their combined efforts hitherto, the firm's reputation was high; its clientele consisted mainly of the titled and landed gentry, who at that time were without doubt the customers to be desired above all others.

Business proceeded on an even keel, with no catastrophic changes: prices were never altered between 1900 and 1914, and the invoice staff knew it by heart; but there was a steady increase of trade. Vintage port was by far their biggest seller. They never in those days bottled more than 18 dozen of sherry at one time; it was condemned by doctors as liverish and bad for diabetics. Claret had gone out of favour before the turn of the century, though it could be had in respectable quality at 18s. a dozen. There was a fair sale for German table wines. Madeira and Marsala were more popular than they are today, especially with Naval officers.

John's sons, Russell and Eddy, having started their apprenticeships in 1883 and 1887 respectively, had now practically ceased to be beginners even by their uncle's standards, and he could rely on their support. It was Eddy's turn in 1908 to visit the United States and Canada. The opportunity came through one of the many outside interests which, like all the Harveys, he found time to cultivate. He was an authority on dogs and used to act as judge at shows. Hence he was asked by an American visitor to get him a pedigree Airedale. He did so and shipped the dog across to the United States. The recipient was so pleased that he invited Eddy to visit him there and promised to introduce him to likely customers. The offer was accepted, with the result that the flow of orders coming across the Atlantic to Denmark Street increased still further. Both Russell and Eddy also visited Spain and Portugal to see the different methods of wine production practised there and to strengthen the firm's relations with their suppliers.

Their two soldier brothers were back from South Africa— Napier with a D.S.O. and a distinguished career in the Engineers before him; Dick also remained in the army for the time.

Considering these four nephews, did Edward ever regret that he had no sons of his own to receive his share of the "heirloom" to which John had referred in one of his last letters? By that word John had meant much more than good dividends: he had meant knowledge and skill, a tradition handed on from his father and enhanced by their own life-long labours—his and Edward's; the thing which all born craftsmen strive to create and to transmit, by heredity, and by the force of example which is strongest when it passes from father to son. It was to pass—was already passing—to two of John's sons. Edward had two children: they were of course much younger than their cousins, since he had married late, and they were girls. They would never be heirs to the tradition.

The balance was redressed in time; for the girls grew up and married, and today Edward's line is represented in the firm by a son-in-law and two grandsons.

In that first decade of the century Denmark Street kept its courtly Victorian forms. All letters of any importance were written by the directors, in their own hand, and copied by clerks into letter books. Long credit was the rule; distinguished clients could not be expected to pay on the nail—it would be beneath their dignity and the firm's—and Russell, having once in a fit of zeal, inspired perhaps by precedents from a time when things were otherwise, written to hasten payment of a long overdue account, was told he must never do such a thing again.

There was no advertising until 1908: the business expanded simply by recommendation or introduction from one client to another. All wine bottles were hand-made, the majority being supplied by Powell & Ricketts of Bristol—successors of the Ricketts who nearly a century before filed the first patent for moulded bottles; Harvey's had an account with them for over a hundred years. Bottling was still done by hand; and to bottle two hogsheads of claret in a day was considered good going by two men. Corks, which were hand cut, were selected to fit the bottle before they were driven in with the beater; then they were dipped in wax and impressed with a seal containing the merchant's name and the designation of the wine. No capsules were used, and no labels: bottles were distinguished by the colour of the seal and by coloured tapes.

Local deliveries were made by a horse-drawn "float". The horse was an old and valued member of the staff and knew his own job as well as anyone; so well that if the driver was delayed at one house the van would punctually move on to the next without him. This led to some embarrassments, for horse, van and contents were sometimes taken in charge by the police, the horse being unable to establish his bona fides. On one occasion delivery was to be made at the house of a clergyman, who was entertaining a teetotal conference, and had wisely given instructions that the van should go to the back. By some oversight this was not explained to the horse, who— the driver leaving navigation to him by force of habit—took the front drive as usual and drew up outside the window, displaying his employer's name and the nature of their merchandise to the assembled company.

Yet already there were signs of change. A typewriter had

appeared in the office by 1900, introduced by a young man
named Wright. Mr. Wright died recently, having completed
well over fifty years' service with the firm and risen to be a
director (29). But at that time he was the junior member of
the staff, having been engaged in February, 1897, on one
month's probation at eighteen shillings a week; and it must
have taken some courage to produce the revolutionary
machine. Edward Harvey, who always wrote with a quill,
remarked when he saw it: "Why don't you use the hands
God gave you?" The horse and "float" passed away in
time: they were found, during one of Bristol's special fogs,
marooned somewhere perilously near the edge of the Avon
Gorge, and were replaced by a motor vehicle.

Edward Harvey was churchwarden at St. Augustine's.
His nephews, Russell and Eddy, supported the church in
Leigh Woods which their father had helped to build. They
both sang in the choir, for which they were coached by Mr.
Wright who was a gifted organist. Russell and his sister
Jean were both married in that church. Jean Harvey's
marriage—to William Garnett, who was also to play an
important part in the firm's story—was the first to be
solemnized there.

The stories of Edward Harvey which have been handed
down show an intriguing mixture of kindliness, unshakable
dignity and dry humour. There was one young recruit to the
staff who, though attracted by the firm's good name,
evidently thought that they were fortunate in having
acquired his services. The Chief was not oblivious and, when
he decided that the time was ripe, prepared to administer his
rebuke thus:

"Ah, Mr. Smith, where is that paper I gave you?"

"On my desk."

"Where?"

"On my desk."

"Be pleased to understand that the paper is on the desk
which you are highly privileged to use for Harvey's."

Another junior, a keen cricketer, was chosen to play for his
club's first eleven one Saturday afternoon. The previous
Monday he asked the Chairman's permission to leave the
office at 1.30 p.m. on the day of the match, the usual Saturday
closing time being two o'clock. But this was far too soon for a

decision to be taken on such a matter. "Be pleased to speak
to me later in the week, say Thursday." On Thursday it
appeared that, since no one knew how important the orders
due on Saturday might be, it would be wiser to postpone
decision until the day. At 11.30 on Saturday the Chairman
was not to be found. After a vain search the young man, in
desperation, changed into his flannels and left promptly at
1.30. Immediately the Chairman appeared and the one
person he wanted was the cricketer. He in turn was hunted for,
high and low, but of course was not found, and no one knew
what had become of him. On Monday morning the Chairman
sought him out.

"Ah, Mr. Jones, what time did you leave on Saturday?"

"At 1.30, sir."

"For what?"

"To play cricket, sir."

"To play cricket! Be pleased to remember that your work
is not done until my work is done . . . and my work is never
done."

That was his way with all juniors. It was never too soon to
inculcate the great virtues—industry, patience, sobriety,
honesty; and above all to implant a true sense of the importance of their work and the great privilege they enjoyed in
serving the firm. "Would not many a gentleman pay a
premium to have his son taught what you have the opportunity to learn?" (That was very true.) His favourite parting
shot at the end of these talks had a characteristic note:
". . . And be pleased to understand that if I say a thing is so
it is so, even if it isn't so."

With senior men he could be lenient. All virtues are subject to temptation, and none more so, in the particular
circumstances of Denmark Street, than sobriety. In spite of
strict rules and their employers' example there were very
occasional lapses. The head clerk at the time, an old and
faithful servant of the firm, appeared one day in such a condition that the others, loyally seeking to conceal the fact from
the approaching Chairman, put him bodily into a large cupboard. Unfortunately he gave his presence away by a loud
snore and all was revealed. Edward Harvey betrayed no
outraged feelings in front of subordinates, but simply sent the
man home in a cab. Another offender was Sherer, an aged

man who had been allowed to keep his employment, which
was to sweep the passage and office entrance, far beyond the
allotted span. Sometimes as he swept he could be seen sway-
ing to and fro, supporting himself on the handle of the broom.
One evening the Chairman passed on his way out and Sherer
saluted him, relinquishing his main support to do so, and thus
giving clear evidence of the state of affairs.

"Sherer," the Chairman said, "you are drunk. You are
dismissed."

"Yes, sir," said Sherer, and went on sweeping.

Next morning he was at work as usual. The Chairman went
straight up to him.

"Sherer, I dismissed you last night for being drunk."

"Yes, sir," Sherer answered humbly, "but you didn't mean
it."

He remained in the firm's employment for some time after
this and died at the ripe age of ninety.

Edward Harvey's chairmanship lasted ten years. His
contribution to the "heirloom" was as great as John's, though
different. His knowledge of wine, according to many who
knew both brothers, was unequalled; and he passed it on without reserve to his nephews. Most of his letters unfortunately
were lost in the bombing of 1940, though he carefully saved
many of those he received from his brother. There remain
some small books kept in his meticulous hand: one or two are
diaries of continental tours; the remainder are tasting notes,
which show even to the uninitiated a keen perception. There
is something poetic in his terse analyses. In the office and
cellars in Denmark Street he left a lasting impression, a
standard of work which could be called strict if it did not
deserve some warmer title; a devotion to the trade as an art
which extended even to small details of routine.

In the city his activities were many. He was a Councillor
for eighteen years, churchwarden, chairman of the Bellringers,
President of the Bristol Madrigal Society, organiser of music
festivals, a Governor of Clifton College, and commander of a
company of the Volunteers; an amateur of astronomy; a keen
supporter of the Shakespeare Society and the Gloucester
County Cricket Club. He died in 1910, having served the
firm for fifty-four years—exactly the same period as his
brother.

The Old Order Changes

Russell—the third John Harvey—now became Chairman (25). His was a strenuous period. England's cheerful careless-ness of a few years ago was wearing thin as more signs of trouble appeared in Europe. Russell himself was a man of strong ideas. He represented a younger generation, although he had been in the business for twenty-seven years. He had shown from the start a disposition to think for himself; and he had had time for thought. A warning of things to come was the fact that Russell did not wear a straw hat in the office. Eddy always did so: it suited his character.

John and Edward had both been devoted to wine as an art. They loved their work, they prospered and were content. Finance for them had taken second place. In fact the firm was in none too sound a position by the strictest standards of finance, though its goodwill was an incalculable asset. Now, with business expanding and a prospect of changing condi-tions, the moment had come for organization. The old tradi-tions were of course still the essence of the trade, and always would be; but something further was necessary to preserve tradition in a new age. Fresh capital was brought in. It was provided by William Garnett, a wealthy man who was Russell Harvey's brother-in-law, having married his sister Jean. He became a director of Harvey's, though he was not an expert on wines and did not concern himself with the technical side of the business; he acted as financial adviser. His support and guidance made it possible to expand and at the same time to keep closer control and to minimize risks. A régime of strict economy began in the office: no one could buy a pen without Mr. Russell's signature on the order.

The firm had begun to advertise in 1908; in which they were pioneers among wine merchants. At first results scarcely justified the expenditure; but Russell was not the man to give up without a proper trial, and in time advertising proved a good investment. Next, the century-old link with Kidderminster was reinforced: Charles Harvey & Company were taken over and became a subsidiary of the Bristol firm.

In October, 1912, the *Wine and Spirit Trade Record* published an article under the title "A Famous Bristol House". The writer had visited Denmark Street and was lucky enough to have a long chat with both brothers, the one a cultured gentleman of the Balfourian type, the other more of the happy-go-lucky, dare-devil, Winston Churchill type. The former gave me a digest of the firm's history; the latter guided me through cellar after cellar until I began to think that instead of being at Bristol I must be at Rheims or Mayence.

That is as good a description as we could wish for of Russell and Eddy Harvey. It must, however, be added of Russell that—cultured gentleman as he was, and strict as he had to be to complete the hard task he had set himself—he had the Harvey streak of humour. At one time there was a controversy in the local Press on the question: What is the national musical instrument of England? After a month or so, when every conceivable instrument had been advocated, Russell sent his contribution to the editor:

Sir:
The national musical instrument of England is the Trumpet
—everyone blowing his own.
Yours in full blast,
J. G. R. Harvey.

By this time the youngest brother, Captain Dick Harvey, had left the army and joined the firm, "turning his sword into a corkscrew" as he put it, and bringing with him another innovation which would have startled his father and uncle— a lady secretary. He visited Canada in 1912. But his stay with the firm was short, as he was on the Reserve of Officers and within a few years another and greater war had claimed him. He commanded a battalion in France and was killed at Hill Sixty.

Bristol, which was now without question a leading port once more, made its full contribution to ultimate victory; its aeroplane factory produced the famous "Bristol" fighter which distinguished itself in the closing stages of the war.

The staff at Denmark Street worked overtime to supply the British Expeditionary Force and naval and military messes in every theatre of war. Cases stencilled with the name of Harvey were found on the battlefields, and some of their wines went through the battle of Jutland in the flagship *Lion*: one bottle of hunting port was the only perishable thing in the wardroom that survived the bombardment, and was later returned to the firm by Admiral Beatty. A big demand came from the military hospitals for red bordeaux and burgundy, the usual prescription for patients suffering from loss of blood at a time when blood transfusion was not organized as it is now. The United States and Canada, where a representative of the firm made another visit during the war, were only too willing to take many times more than could be sent to them.

Though the work was exhausting, total sales dropped while duties increased. Lloyd George's famous and detested D.O.R.A. compelled pre-payment for wines and spirits; which may have evoked a wry smile from Russell if he remembered the rebuke he had once received for trying to hasten an overdue account. The influx of ready money was something of an embarrassment to the firm, which had been accustomed to operate on the basis of twelve months' credit.

Though Bristol port was as busy as it has ever been, its imports of wine decreased by more than half in the last year of the war. This was partly owing to government restrictions and partly to loss of shipping: in June, 1917, the *Sir Walter*, owned by the Bristol shippers, Turner, Edwards & Company, which had done faithful service for many years in carrying wine from Portugal, was sunk by a German submarine.

The end of the war found stocks of wine in Bristol sadly depleted; the Denmark Street cellars were all but empty. There followed a frantic period of re-stocking, which brought the wine imports of Bristol for the next two years to a fantastic figure, many times greater than the pre-war maximum; even the totals that followed the Second World War, when imports were under better control, did not approach the peak of 1919. Ships poured in from Bordeaux, Oporto, Cadiz, Lisbon, Valencia; though so far as Harvey's were concerned it was now French wines—claret and burgundy—that were stocked in the greatest quantities.

Casks of wine were piled in the roadways from near the back of the Cathedral almost to the Gasworks Ferry, obstructing traffic and inviting the attentions of looters—a menace to peace and good order, so that the police had to guard them day and night; and Turner, Edwards & Company, the shippers, were reluctantly compelled to divert some of their shipments to Newport. The dock authorities were criticized—unfairly, since the influx was abnormal—for failing to provide accommodation. There were some sharp exchanges between them, the police and the shippers, until at length a bonded warehouse became available and the tempting casks disappeared from the public eye.

By this time there had been another change in the Harvey chairmanship. The reorganization and the war had resulted in nine years of continuous and abnormal strain, and Russell Harvey was not one to spare himself. He was so crippled by arthritis that a baluster had been rigged to help him down the stairs to the cellars. In 1919, when illness kept him away from the office for a time, Eddy said one day to Mr. Wright, who was now a trusted lieutenant and secretary of the company: "We shan't see Mr. Russell again." No one else had realized how bad things were: it was a great shock to everyone when Russell died suddenly shortly afterwards. He was only fifty-six, but had spent thirty-six of those years in the service of Harvey's.

The full value of his contribution was never apparent to him, nor to anyone during his lifetime. In the past nine years, though perhaps no one realized the fact as yet, the world in which he had grown up had vanished for ever. He had seen the necessity for certain changes in the firm's structure, and had carried them out with great courage. They were important at the time; but they were far more essential in the changed world which gradually revealed itself after his death. He had acted more wisely than he could have known.

During his chairmanship the firm's strength had been increased by two more personalities who were to play a large part in the future. A young man named Cox came in as the junior member of the staff in 1914, in time to know some of the generation who had served under John Harvey the second, such as Henry Hodge and Albert Nelmes, and to absorb the traditions and stories handed down from the unforgettable years before the turn of the century. He became a director in 1945 and has since completed forty years' service. Besides his great knowledge of the trade and the art of wine, he is an inexhaustible well of facts—both serious and comical—concerning the firm's earlier days.

The second addition was Sutton Bendle (29). He was an older man and had been a partner in Hope & Bendle, wine merchants, of Carlisle. How the Government took over the liquor trade in Carlisle during the 1914 war, and established the famous State-managed inns, is a well-known story. Sutton Bendle was soon tired of being, as he expressed it, a Government servant; and when in 1917 Russell Harvey, already handicapped by arthritis, asked him to come to Bristol as general manager and to share the burdens of war-time, he gladly accepted. He also in time was given a seat on the Board, and later was responsible for starting the firm's London office. He died in 1945.

So during Russell Harvey's chairmanship—by a small margin the shortest in the firm's history—many steps were taken which profoundly influenced the future.

CHÂTEAU D'YQUEM

CHAPTER IX

New Times, New Ways

JOHN HARVEY the fourth—John St. Clair Harvey: "Mr.
Jack" already to everyone at Denmark Street, where
they were quite accustomed to adopting new variants on
familiar Christian names—was a schoolboy at Harrow as his
father had been. He had looked forward to some extensive
travelling now that the world was at peace, and then to
Oxford. Russell's early death and the needs of the business
put a sudden end to all that: he came into the firm at once as
an apprentice at £60 a year. He had a long way to go before
he could be considered qualified for the chairmanship which
had never been held by anyone with less than twenty years'
experience in the firm. His own period of preparation was to
last nineteen years.

Now, however, as always, there was a Harvey ready to
take over, and as thoroughly groomed for the office as any of
his predecessors. John the second had been succeeded by his
brother Edward; John the third—Russell—was now succeeded by his brother Eddy—the "happy-go-lucky, dare-
devil, Winston Churchill type" (27). The change was one of
those tricks of appropriateness which fortune sometimes
plays. Russell's vision, courage and tact had carried the burden through the darkest days. Peace and high hopes for the
world—illusory though they might prove—were well fitted
by Eddy's irrepressible nature. A particular brand of the
Harvey humour was his special characteristic; he was a wit.
But he also had charm, and enormous knowledge of the
business, and such an inborn love of it that even when he was
very old, and had handed over the reins to his nephew,
nothing could keep him away from Denmark Street. If his
straw hat signified a determined championship of the old ways,
that too was right. Russell's reforms were accomplished; and
tradition is, after all, the acknowledged foundation of the trade.

The new Chairman's conservatism showed itself when the progressive cellar manager laid before the Board his plans and estimates for modernization of bottling methods. He was listened to with close attention, and searching questions born of experience were asked and answered. After long discussion the directors were equally divided between "pro" and "con". The Chairman must give the casting vote. But at that precise moment the Chairman found it necessary to leave the boardroom. "A tactful move," said one. "Yes," said the others, "but we will wait for him. He must decide." After some minutes the Chairman returned and calmly asked whether the matter was settled.

"No," said his nephew. "We are waiting for your decision."

"Very well," said the Chairman, and turned to address the cellar manager. "We have to thank you for your interest in the production of our wines. We realize the sales are increasing and the rate of bottling must be improved. We value all the investigations you have made to this end, and thank you for the drawings submitted, but you can do what you like when I am dead."

Eddy's humour could be compared with Edward's as two sherries—the uncle's dry, the nephew's towards the other extreme. There was a warehouseman who added to his income by acting at cheap shows as a female impersonator, and used to practise his art during working hours. His wailing contralto often pierced the calm of the office, and one day reached the ears of the Chairman, who put on his straw hat and went to seek the cause of the disturbance. Standing out of sight of the singer, he shouted, "Clara Butt, shut up," and returned to the office. The man said indignantly to his mates: "What a bloomin' cheek, and me topping the bill tonight at the Pig and Whistle!" But he was silenced.

In his younger days Eddy was a stickler for neatness in handwriting, and set the office junior, whom he considered lacking in this virtue, to copy his own hand—than which, at least in his own opinion, there could be no better model. The young man complied, and improved so much that nearly forty years later the Chairman complimented him on his writing. He was duly grateful, and reminded the Chief of his advice which he had long since forgotten.

28 John St. Clair Harvey, the present Chairman

27 Eddy Harvey, Chairman from 1919 to 1937

29 Eddy Harvey's Jubilee, 7th July, 1937. In the front row are
(left to right) J. St. Clair Harvey, Eddy Harvey, Mrs. Eddy Harvey,
Sutton Bendle and B. G. T. Wright

30 150th Anniversary Celebrations, 1946

"Well, well," said the old gentleman. "That must account
for my overdraft."

Eddy spent much of his spare time in his workshop and
garden, and often on Saturday afternoons in summer two of
the warehousemen were invited to his home as helpers. They
generally accepted with pleasure, for the old gentleman was
kind and generous, and there were many incidents which on
Monday morning filled the cellars with laughter. One Saturday the task was to water the flower beds. Water was fetched
from a well some half-mile from the house in a milk churn
mounted on a crank-axle cart which was drawn by a donkey.
With due ceremony the turn-out and its driver set off; but it
failed to return. The Chairman, looking across the fields, saw
the donkey rooted to the ground and the unfortunate driver
doing everything he could to persuade it to move, but without
avail. The man pulled, pushed and beat, but the animal
refused to budge. The Chairman knew a better way. He
walked across, lifted the donkey's ear and shouted into it one
word: "Home!" At once it set off at such a pace that the two
elderly men came panting behind.

Not all the stories told of Eddy Harvey are comic. One
tells of an employee who was found by Mr. Cox in a state of
acute depression: he had furnished his home on the hire
purchase system and now could not pay the instalments. Mr.
Cox told the Chairman and was sent to inquire the extent of
the debt, which turned out to be £40. Eddy made out a cheque
for that amount, then asked the man's permission to take two
shillings a week from his wages for repayment. When
Christmas time came there was no Christmas box for that
man. It was a sore disappointment until he was told that his
outstanding debt to the firm—some £39, allowing for the
weekly payments—had been forgiven.

Eddy Harvey was a gentleman of the good old-fashioned
type; yet it was his lot to control the business at a time when
many old ideas and standards had gone for ever. Evidence of
change appeared in the firm's accounts. Cellars were being
sold off; people wanted the money for other uses; they wanted
to spend it. The motor-car had arrived. Life was less static
and no longer anchored to the family home. There were
fewer big dinner-parties in private houses, more restaurant
meals. Less wine was sold by the pipe for laying down, more

to caterers and, through wholesalers, to people who liked to buy a bottle or two when they wanted it. This trend was indirectly increased by the advertising, from 1918 onwards, of sample cases, which created a whole new class of customers —people who bought a little at a time in the modern manner, and, though firmly loyal henceforth to the name of Harvey's, found it more convenient to deal with their local merchant. In the face of this insistent demand the local merchant was virtually compelled to stock Harvey's wines, and the firm could scarcely refuse to supply him. Thus an ancient tradition—private customers only—was broken down perforce, and soon Harvey's travellers were covering the country from end to end.

During the 'twenties the sales of sherry, which had been recovering, fell off again. This was owing to the cocktail habit —a deplorable thing in Harvey's opinion, for it ruins the finer perceptions of the palate which are essential for the enjoyment of table wines during the meal. They believe that sherry's return to popularity was chiefly thanks to women, many of whom found cocktails too potent and strong in taste; though it was owing partly to the fact that sherry shippers woke early in the morning and advertised, while the port shippers slept. It was sometime in the 'thirties—no exact details can be given, for the records were destroyed by enemy action—that the firm's sales of sherry first exceeded those of port.

Bristol's wine imports suffered a reaction from the wild re-stocking boom of 1919–20; but two years later they were climbing again. By 1925 they were far greater than they had ever been before the war. In the same year the total tonnage of shipping entered from foreign ports passed the two million mark.

Harvey's had lost, for the time, two very valued customers when the United States went "dry" in 1919 and Canada followed province by province. (Quebec, with its huge French population, only stood prohibition for a year and then went "wet" again, though purchasing was in the hands of a Liquor Control Board.) Despite the temporary loss of these markets the volume of business continued to increase. Advertising, now an important part of the firm's policy, proved its value. The original cellar, plus the additions provided by John the second and further extensions made from time to time, formed, with their connecting passages, a network that stretched out under the neighbouring streets and buildings: yet there was little room to spare. Huge casks stood one above another, the upper tiers scarcely visible in the dim light, among the pendent filaments of dark red wine-gossamer: the bins, each marked with a designation and a date, held thousands of bottles, cradled on their sides like stone knights in an ancient church—but living, asleep, preparing unhurriedly for the day of their perfection. It might seem that time had forgotten these vaults. Yet there was constant movement. Empty casks—sad shells, the soul departed—were carried off; fresh casks, gravid with goodness, were borne in from the Customs' bonded warehouse and laid to rest on the scantlings; bottles were roused and packed off to the consummation of their dreams—to give forth in an hour the sunlight of months on a southern hillside. The cellarmen walked with hushed feet in that place, but they were certainly busy.

Evolution had been at work in the office above. Clerks no longer copied letters into letter-books; and Mr. Wright's typewriter had changed its status from novelty to museum piece. In the cellars too: "Mr. Jack", performing the proper role of the younger generation, had seen the first labelling machine at the Brewers' Exhibition; it was purchased and installed. Next to appear was a machine for fitting capsules; then a filling machine. Eddy Harvey's conservatism was perhaps something of a pose, for the firm were pioneers of mechanical bottling; and they found that it saved not only labour and time but also space—another valuable commodity, much in demand for larger and larger stocks.

Machines, of course, have nothing to do with the essential processes of production—the growing of grapes, the making and maturing of wine. The sacred rites are performed as they always have been, except where methods may be modified—with due reverence and cautious trial—by fresh knowledge. Mechanical devices are applied under strict supervision to the less vital services, where they can increase efficiency without prejudicing art. The Denmark Street cellars are equipped with electric light (with gas too, for Edward Harvey had insisted on its retention because of its effect on temperature); but when wine is drawn from the cask it is greeted and probed by the rays of a candle, which alone, the experts say, bring its nature to light and reveal its true condition.

A word here about the special methods by which the two most famous of all Harvey's sherries, Bristol Cream and Bristol Milk, are produced. Certain fine sherries are brought to Bristol from several different sources in Spain. Each has already been aged in cask in its native country, and skilfully blended by the *solera* system which is designed to maintain the individual standard of quality and style. From these the final blend is composed in the firm's own cellars. How it is done is Harvey's secret.

The Chairman's nephew, "Mr. Jack", was now the firm's chief ambassador overseas (28). He went to France in 1919, to Spain in 1920, and in 1921 to Portugal with Sutton Bendle. In 1928 he was in Canada, where prohibition had been dying by degrees. This visit took him right across the continent. One evening he was in the Empress Hotel, Victoria, with a business friend and a lady. A dance was going on and it was suggested that, if another lady could be found, they might join in. With true hospitality they asked Jack Harvey what sort of partner he would prefer. He thought quickly and replied: "Blonde, a good dancer, with a sense of humour." A lady answering this description was produced—Miss Tolmie, daughter of Dr. Simon Tolmie, then premier of British Columbia. The evening was a success. So, evidently, was the lady; for in 1930 she became Mrs. Jack Harvey, and in due course mother of the child whom all the family guardian angels acclaimed as John Harvey the fifth.

In December, 1933, the United States, after fourteen years' chastening experience, went "wet" again, and the golden age of gangsterdom was over. In Bristol, England, the staff of John Harvey & Sons worked day and night, packing, labelling, despatching and invoicing. There had never been anything like the flood of orders. Some months later the Park & Tilford Distillers Corporation of New York became Harvey's agents in the United States. From that time, with their invaluable support, and a biennial visit (the war years excepted) by the Chairman, the firm's American and Canadian trade has gone from strength to strength. The directors saw the special conditions existing in these countries, which are clearly summarized here in their own words:

31 St. James's Square, London, *c.* 1710. Harvey's London Office
is situated on the corner of King Street—the turning off the
left side of the square

From an engraving by Sutton Nicholls

32 Portsmouth Dockyard in 1841, from the Hard, where Harvey's
premises are situated

From a contemporary engraving

33 S.S. *Starling* on the River Avon below the Clifton Suspension Bridge. The ship brings many cargoes of wine to Harvey's

Owing to the period of prohibition, a generation grew up in America, and Canada to a lesser degree, that had little or no knowledge of the delights and benefits of wine. Canada re-explored these possibilities first as their prohibition period was shorter-lived than that of America.

During prohibition, what the drinking public required if they could get it was "a shot of alcohol", and consequently spirits in some form or other were the quickest and most convenient answer.

However, both countries now appear to be becoming more and more appreciative of imported Sherries and Ports, although the proportion of sales is 10 of Sherry to 1 of Port.

Climatically, spirits have an advantage over wines in these two countries—long drinks with a spirit basis in the hot summer, and strong short drinks with the same basis in the cold seasons.

However, with the abundance of good food available there is still every hope of persuading more and more Americans and Canadians that the appreciation of a meal can be enhanced enormously by preceding it or accompanying it with wine rather than spirits.

At the same time Harvey's were strengthening their position nearer home. Between 1927 and 1932 they opened branches in Malta, Devonport and Chatham. In 1933 the Portsmouth branch was joined with the century-old firm of Stokes & Company (one of whose catalogues has been quoted) to form Stokes & Harvey, at 15 and 16, The Hard; and the Cardiff firm of Hunt, Wightwick and Company Limited was taken over: both these later became branches of John Harvey & Sons. They, with Charles Harvey & Company of Kidderminster, represent three of Bristol's historic inland trade connections—the West Midlands, the South Coast and Wales. In 1934 Sutton Bendle went to London to take charge of the new London office at 4a King Street, Saint James's. A Glasgow branch was opened in 1937.

Among its treasured mementoes of a long connection with the Navy, the Portsmouth branch has an almost complete collection of Navy Lists, the earlier numbers taken over from Stokes & Company. This begins with "A List of the Flag Officers of His Majesty's Fleet with the dates of their first commissions". It is dated July, 1797, and includes among Rear-Admirals of the Blue the name of Sir Horatio Nelson,

K.B. The next is the first of "Steel's original and correct list
of the Royal Navy corrected to November, 1800".

End—and Beginning

Eddy Harvey retired when he had completed his fifty
years' service with the firm, in 1938. That is to say, he vacated
the chairmanship, which was the nearest any Harvey had
ever come to retiring except when his uncle Charles (not, of
course, his great uncle, Charles Harvey of Kidderminster)
severed his connection as a young man some eighty years
before. Eddy sought to postpone even this step by a whim-
sical subterfuge which was characteristic of him, pretending
that there had been a mistake about the date of his joining,
and so putting off from month to month the impending
jubilee. However, the day came. He remained a director,
and continued to appear daily at Denmark Street—still
wearing his straw hat, making his jokes, and beloved by
everyone—and to give his successor the benefit of his vast
knowledge, until he died in 1950.

So, when the Second World War broke over Europe, control
of the firm's affairs was in the hands of the fourth John
Harvey. The tragedy of his father's early death had this
good effect—that in the new Chairman, as in his predecessors,
whatever heredity has to give in the way of instinct was now
reinforced by the solid experience of twenty years.

Bristol was a key port in the conduct of the war. Vital
shipping was transferred from the east coast, which was more
exposed to enemy attack, to the west, and in those six crucial
years 41 million tons of goods passed through Bristol. Hundreds of factories turned over to war materials and munitions.
The works that had been responsible for the historic "Bristol"
fighter now produced the "Blenheim" bomber and later the
"Beaufighter", in its time the fastest two-engined aircraft.
The importance of Bristol in the war effort drew upon it the
attentions of the *Luftwaffe*. Night after night, in the opera-
tions rooms of the Royal Air Force and Anti-Aircraft Command, those sinister arrows that represented hostile aircraft
crept silently across the map in the same direction, and duty
officers muttered: "Bristol again." Half the shops on Park
Street disappeared in the first year, leaving broken stumps
and mounds of rubble which time mercifully masked with

purple willow-herb. Districts round the centre, so near the vital docks, were almost completely flattened.

The Chairman had rejoined his regiment in the early days of the war. Sutton Bendle came back to help in Bristol, leaving the London office in other hands. One morning in November, 1940, he and Eddy Harvey, coming down as usual, found a police cordon drawn around Denmark Street, and as they hurried through they heard a constable say: "Harvey's is flat." It very nearly was. The old house, home of the business for close on 150 years, was a smoking ruin. Historic records, the visitors' book with its unique collection of autographs, current accounts, treasured glass, personal belongings and precious relics—all were gone, along with the contents of a warehouse that had been stacked to the roof. Eddy's buoyant old heart was nearly broken.

The cellars, thanks to the stout work of medieval masons, were intact, though the great oak door was destroyed. The rubble was cleared from the entrance; a little old house in a narrow neighbouring street, Pipe Lane, was taken to serve as temporary headquarters; and the business carried on. In April, 1941, the London office was "blitzed". It was moved to another address, which in turn was bombed in February, 1944.

There is no need to dwell on war-time difficulties, which were of the same nature as hundreds of British firms were facing; though, looking back, one wonders where the spirit came from that carried them through. It was not the young and the strong who bore that burden through the long, dark days and the nights that were sometimes too brightly lit. The Chairman was seconded from his regiment to M.I.5 as a security officer in south-west Wales, and throughout the war he had very little time to give to the business. Eddy was an old man now. It was "young" Mr. Wright (he had forty-two years' service behind him so far) who shouldered the chief responsibility. Luckily he had two able supporters. Mr. Cox had followed the same road as himself, beginning as office junior; he had served the firm through one world war already and was no novice, even by Harvey's standards, after over a quarter-century under Eddy's tutorship. At this time he took over the cellar management. Sutton Bendle—slightly his junior in service with the firm though older in years and length of experience in the trade—was a tremendous help in those difficult times. He did not return to London but stayed at the Pipe Lane headquarters, a wonderfully young man for his years—he still took a swim every day—until his death early in 1945. He is remembered as a very charming and courteous gentleman, with a passion for order and cleanliness.

In the first two years of this war more wine came into Bristol than ever before except in the corresponding years of the previous war. The merchants, foreseeing import restrictions, were stocking all they could. Besides this, some wine ships were wrecked off the south-west coast, and parts of their cargoes found their way into Bristol. Then the expected Government restrictions came. In 1942 the port handled 50 tons of wine and spirits as against nearly 9,500 tons in 1941. For the next three years the average was about 400 tons. Harvey's struggled to meet the demand from shrinking stocks, giving what preference they could to Service messes. It was extra hard work for a pathetically small result. Towards the end Mr. Wright and his helpers just managed to keep the business going.

After the Crisis

Victory found Bristol sadly battered, some of its finest old buildings wrecked beyond hope of repair, and its wine trade reduced to a fraction of the peace-time normal. But the obstinate spirit which one of the agitators had denounced had its admirable side. In spite of shortage of building materials and skilled labour, thousands of new houses have appeared, brighter, more spacious, more modern—though perhaps less romantic to our eyes—than those which were destroyed. In the City Centre, where once ships pushed up the Frome through the old drawbridge, new Corporation 'buses circulate smoothly round islands made of lawns and flowers; and an enlarged College Green sets off the old Cathedral in all its dignity, flanked by a huge arc of new municipal buildings on whose topmost gables a pair of golden unicorns posture defiantly. These latest symbols of Bristol's vitality stand high in the air; their horns seem to prick the clouds: yet above them still rise two towers—the modern Gothic of the university, and Cabot's memorial.

The old diversity of manufactures has been maintained.

34 The old premises, destroyed in 1940 by enemy bombing

35 The new offices, on the site of the old, opened in 1954

DENMARK STREET

36 The Main Cellar in Denmark Street

37 Mr. G. Long, the
head bottler, at work
in the cellars

Though sugar-refining and glass have gone, the craft of pottery flourishes still: but the main emphasis has shifted to engineering, from special gears and box-making machines to a highly distinguished motor-car, the "Bristol" two-litre, the "Britannia" air liner, and the enormously powerful "Olympus" jet engine.

The port with its great docks, the largest municipally-owned docks in Britain, has played its proper part in the export drive. It is equipped with modern aids—diesel locomotives and electric trucks and cranes—for rapid movement of merchandise and quick turn-round of ships: it showed what can be done when a cargo of 633 tractors for overseas was loaded and stowed in six and a half hours. Its pilots and dockers are second to none, for their business is in the blood from generations back.

As to imports, tobacco, cocoa and chocolate are manufactured and marketed all over the world by Bristol firms. Timber and grain come from Canada; meat, dairy produce and zinc ore from the Antipodes. Colonies of oil storage tanks, like huge metal beehives, cluster round Avonmouth. The total of shipping entering Bristol docks in 1945 was over four million tons. Yet modern Bristol is rich in reminders of the past out of which it grew. Its churches remain, though a few are blackened ruins, and the Chamber of Commerce meets in the room where the Bristol Free Port Association used to meet in the 1840's—the room that may have been Edward Colston's banqueting hall.

Harvey's had one piece of luck in their efforts to meet the immediate post-war demand at home while imports were still restricted. About half of the extensive stocks they held in 1939 had been earmarked for export. These were prevented by the war from reaching their intended destination—a blessing in disguise, for they were switched to the home market; otherwise the firm would have had to close its doors. As it was, they tided over until supplies returned to normal, which they did very quickly. Bristol's wine imports had almost equalled the pre-war figure by 1947. In the next three years they were more than doubled, and in 1951 reached a new record apart from the freak figures produced by the two world wars.

In the Denmark Street cellars, as in Bristol city, the new

rubs shoulders with the old. Here, while sherry is drawn from the butt by candle-light, the ghosts of the first John Harvey and his two sons and two grandsons, grouped in the flickering shadow between cask and buttress, watch with amazement—and perhaps some inarticulate regret—the machines that fill, capsule, label and pack an endless succession of bottles. Upstairs, they marvel at the busy typewriters and the new accounting methods. To their practised eyes the sales records tell a story of social change. No longer do large orders from the stately homes of the rich—pipes of port and hogsheads of claret for laying down—figure as they did fifty years ago; a far greater part consists of dozens or even lesser lots. These are the customers who matter most today; a vast market, whose growing numbers more than compensate for smaller purchasing power. And, though the private client is always specially valued and respected, it has become necessary to provide through wholesalers and caterers for the *ad hoc* buyer and for those who consume their wines while lunching or dining in restaurants.

There are signs, too, of widening discrimination and desire for knowledge among the public. The present Harvey directors know this as well as anyone. Those who come to them for guidance are numbered in thousands; and their enquiries are always welcome even though the resulting orders, taken singly, are often small. A modest budget, and determination to get the best value from it, are the best of reasons for thoughtful choice based on sound advice. Surprisingly often, though perhaps they can only afford a little, people will buy what John Harvey the second used to call "the pearls": and Harvey's, well aware of the situation, take special pains to provide for them really good wines at prices that are within their reach. They have proved that this can be done by great care in selection. There has never been, they say, a wider appreciation of good wine; what is needed is wider knowledge, and that they are doing their best to propagate. As to price, the position of table wines was greatly improved by Sir Stafford Cripps's reduction of duties in 1949, though a further reduction would pay dividends in the end by increasing consumption. Hotels and restaurants should make a determined effort to bring down their prices— now the chief bar to more general enjoyment. Why should we be denied, through false austerity or mistaken policies, the best of all accompaniments to good food and good company?

The cocktail habit, though not extinct, is no longer as widespread as it was, and has ceased to menace that supreme *apéritif*, sherry. Sherry has more than recovered its position, lost and regained so often in history. Even Russell Harvey, the present Chairman's father, would be surprised to find it predominating over port, which suffers unduly not only from high duties (vintage port, which you could lay down in 1908 at 42s. a dozen, now costs 20s. a bottle) but also from the changed pattern of life; its special qualities, designed by Providence for leisurely enjoyment after a good dinner, cannot appeal in the same degree when one must leave the table hurriedly to enable an impatient staff to complete the washing up—or when one has to wash up oneself. South African wines, sherry in particular, have made great strides since the wine farmers of the Union began a concerted effort to improve their products and to popularize them. Yet demand is as healthily varied as ever. The firm's catalogue contains long lists of ports and sherries, burgundies, clarets, champagnes, hocks, moselles, madeiras, and the rest. In its pages the connoisseur can browse and dream, as an angler dreams a winter evening away over his favourite tackle-maker's list; planning, anticipating—or, if he is very poor, indulging in simple fantasy: and even a teetotaller, unless he be quite proof against the magic of sound, will be held and enticed by the music of these names—Musigny, Nuits Saint Georges, Rüdesheimer Roseneck, Château la Croix de Gay.

Those five ghostly critics, conservative though we must suppose them to be, will find many things in the present situation to approve. At first, if celestial newspapers have contained reports of rising prices and taxes and general shortage of cash, they may be anxious about the state of business. The firm's sales figures, showing new record totals, will reassure them; and they will be told that it is nothing unusual nowadays for a ship to enter the city docks with a complete cargo consigned to John Harvey & Sons Limited. Russell will note that his innovation, advertising, has proved its value in the modern world; to meet the demand it has created, Harvey's travellers cover the whole of England,

Scotland and Wales. John the first will be pleased to find a strengthened connection with Kidderminster where he spent ten years of his early life, and the naval business represented by branches at four chief stations of the Fleet, besides other branches in Glasgow and Malta, and a London office established (after its war-time misfortunes) at 40, King Street, St. James's, with two resident directors, G. L. Walker and H. H. Waugh. Edward, when he finds his daughter's husband, Colonel McWatters, and their son among the directors and another grandson in the position of secretary, will feel that time has given him everything he most desired. But if he tries a dignified dig at his brother on this score, John the second will glance at his own grandson, now Chairman, and let it pass. The next generation of John's family too is already there in the person of "Mr. Jack's" daughter Anne, assistant secretary; and the fifth John Harvey, at Harrow—and now Head of the School—will come forward in time, the gods permitting, after due initiation to carry on the line.

Eddy will be interested in the universities; he will be told that senior and junior common rooms are being encouraged in true appreciation by a series of wine tastings—that Harvey's are bringing education in their own special art to the great centres of learning. Regular visits to the wine-growing countries will be taken for granted; though Edward will be charmed to hear from his grandson, George McWatters—a Vintners' Scholar—of tours to the very spots once so familiar to himself, and generous welcomes given by his own host's grandchildren. Russell and Eddy will notice that business trips to the United States and Canada have become a great deal more frequent since their day, and have been for some time a biennial fixture in the Chairman's calendar. He has broken new ground too since the war—South Africa and the Rhodesias in 1947, Bermuda and the West Indies in 1949. None of his ancestors spent a fraction of the time and trouble he has spent in travelling to the buying countries overseas. They will see that his efforts have been repaid; for—in spite of exchange controls and all the barriers with which, as history shows, human beings impede distribution of the earth's good gifts—the books contain active export accounts with nearly a hundred different countries: sales to the United States and Canada alone in 1953 totalled more than

38 The Tunnels—the cellars where vintage wines are stored

39 An old bottle discovered during the re-building of the premises, compared with one of the famous Bristol-shaped bottles of today

40   The retail premises in Denmark Street

41   A corner of the Denmark Street cellars reconstructed as a replica
of a Spanish vineyard scene

£428,000. This is the present outcome of all their labours, a result to which each generation has contributed in its turn.

But what is troubling the five visitors? They are looking round, questioning, as if some essential part of the place were missing. Where are Sutton Bendle and young Mr. Wright? At the sound of the names a sixth and a seventh shade appear and join them. Yes, Mr. Wright too is one of them now. He served for fifty-four years.

Remembering that they all have a sense of humour, we must be sure that they see a certain file of correspondence concerning the historic subject of Bristol Milk. It begins with a letter dated December, 1949, from the Ministry of Food, drawing attention to Regulation One of the Defence (Sales of Food) Regulations, 1943, which makes it an offence to mislead as to the nature, substance and quality of a food, or in particular as to its nutritional or dietary value. "In the Ministry's opinion," it continues, "the use of the wording 'Bristol Milk' might well be held to contravene the said regulations on the ground that this indicates the presence of milk and as such suggests that the wine has certain special nutritive qualities."

The Chairman's reply, after pointing out that the term "Bristol Milk" has been in use for over 300 years, remarks that presumably the same objection would apply "to 'Bristol Cream' and as a result to all shaving creams, hair creams, face creams, boot creams, etc., as suggesting they have a nutritive value". Whether this logic appealed to the officials in London is doubtful; but when it was mentioned that the export trade for these two brands of sherry in America and Canada alone amounted to some 500,000 dollars per annum, their hearts were apparently softened. At any rate Bristol Cream and Bristol Milk still appear in the catalogue; though, like all really good things in these times, they are not very easy to come by, for demand vastly exceeds supply.

This correspondence somehow reached the hands of the local newspapers. It was honoured with editorials, and provoked a flood of letters full of historical instances and quotations; which proves that Bristol citizens have not lost their love of old things nor relinquished their zest for the liquid which, if old Fuller's information was correct, was the first to moisten the infant lips of their ancestors.

Before the seven visitors return to their other world they

must go outside and see what is to be seen. For four of them it will be a cruel shock to find that the ancient house—focus of childhood memories, lifelong labours, and hopes for the next generation; one-time repository of their common heirloom—has vanished.

Well, the past is gone. Though tradition meant much to them, they are all men whose lives were devoted to the future. There will be a message for them in the fine modern building which, since the last of them passed on, has risen from the ashes of the old (35). What will they think of it? What criticisms will it provoke, what praise not easily won, what crusty or comical *mots* on new architectural styles, what deep reflections on the changing course of life? Let them read the inscription carved beside the entrance:

THIS STONE WAS LAID
BY
JOHN ST. CLAIR HARVEY
CHAIRMAN OF
JOHN HARVEY & SONS LIMITED
TO COMMEMORATE THE REBUILDING
OF THE COMPANY'S PREMISES
ON THE TWELFTH ANNIVERSARY OF THE
DESTRUCTION BY ENEMY ACTION
OF THE ORIGINAL BUILDING ON THE
NIGHT OF THE 24TH NOVEMBER 1940.

Then leave them alone to think and to feel what they must.

*   *   *   *

Perhaps the most felicitous comment with which to close this record is one made by Professor Saintsbury, who has already been quoted earlier on, and who was well-known to the present Chairman, a founder-member of the Saintsbury Club, formed to honour the vinous and literary fame of the Professor. In his "Notes on a Cellar-Book" he wrote:

Let me note a wonderful Pedro Ximenes, stamped "Sherry" and furnished to me with the ticket "very old in 1860", by my constant friend in these ways, the late Mr. John Harvey of Bristol, respecting whose cellars and those of his successors it may certainly be said: "there's *nothing* rotten in the *street* of Denmark".

APPENDIX

Some Harvey Wine Lists

O WING to the loss of records in the 1940 bombing, early
wine lists of Harvey's are very rare. However, one of
exceptional interest is in existence, and is reproduced on
page 114. Its date is 1st January, 1867, in the middle of a period
when there was a great revival of wine drinking in England. The
reason for this increase is not far to seek.

Contrary to popular belief today, wine was not cheap in the
nineteenth century. This was partly owing to the high duties on
French wines, which in the Napoleonic Wars rose as high as
19s. 8d. a gallon—over 3s. 3d. a bottle. Subsequently it was
lowered to 5s. 6d. a gallon, but although the population of these
islands was rising sharply, consumption of wine dropped. In the
last decade of the eighteenth century the annual average consumption had been over 6½ million gallons; fifty years later it
was not much more than 6 million, and in the intervening years
had dropped to under 5 million gallons a year.

However, as indicated on page 93, this was all changed by
Gladstone in the years 1860–1862, when as Chancellor of the
Exchequer he accepted the advice of certain leading figures in
the wine trade and by a series of reductions brought the duty on
red and white table wines down to 1s. a gallon—2d. a bottle.
The duties on fortified wines from Portugal and Spain were not
reduced so sharply; they were fixed at 2s. 6d. a gallon. The results
of these changes, which were accompanied by measures making
it possible for almost every grocer and refreshment-house keeper
to sell wine, were startling. By 1861 the imports of wines rose
to 10¾ million gallons, and it continued to rise during the sixties
and seventies. The increase was most marked in French wines,
the average consumption of which in the first sixty years
of the century had averaged not much more than 350,000
gallons a year. But in 1861 they jumped to almost 2¾ million
gallons.

Against this background, the 1867 list of Harvey and White's
may be examined. Like all long-established wine merchants they

were faced with the competition of cheap—and often inferior—
wines sold by the new "Gladstone wine sellers". It is clear that
they were not being rushed into price-cutting or lowering of
quality. The price of fine wine was high, quite apart from the
duty. In 1867 Harvey's were offering the 1864 clarets in cask for
those who—as was not uncommon in those days—either had their
wine bottled at home, or bought a hogshead from their merchant,
who then bottled the 23 dozen for their client; he made a small
saving by such bulk purchase. The wide range of prices may be
noted. Whereas one could buy a hogshead of sound Pauillac for
£26 a hogshead, and paid £48 for the highly respectable Pontet
Canet, to acquire a hogshead of one of the first growths, Lafite
or Latour, would cost £94. (The high prices for claret in the
mid-nineteenth century may be gauged by the fact that in a
1938 list of Harvey's, Lafite and Latour 1934 were offered at 84s.
a dozen, château bottled, practically the same price as the 1864
vintage in the list of 1867. It should be added that claret prices
were abnormally low in the inter-war period; Pontet Canet 1864
was 43s. 10d. a dozen in 1867, while the 1934 vintage was 45s.
in the 1938 list. During the seventy intervening years the value
of money must have depreciated at least three to four times.)
It may be added that Harvey's had obviously chosen well in their
first growths, for the 1864 Lafite is often considered to mark the
high point of pre-phylloxera claret. Among the older wines two
representative of the famous 1858 vintage will be noticed. The
absence of older wines may be ascribed partly to the then general
habit of drinking even fine wines when young and partly to the
bad vintages which followed the devastation of the French vineyards by the oidium, or wine disease, in 1851. This disease,
leading to a scarcity of wines, was also responsible for a rise in
wine prices.

Claret clearly occupies pride of place in the Harvey's list;
burgundy was not so much in demand. Red and white are listed
together, and only seven are offered—as against 33 clarets and
5 white bordeaux. Nor is the dearest red burgundy (Chambertin
1857 at 88s. a dozen) as dear as the 1858 clarets at 92s.—the
reverse of price trends today. The list shows that Château
d'Yquem was then as now always a dear wine. The 1861 vintage
was listed at 126s., as against 66s., for the very reputable Château
Suduiraut of the same year. Only one or two of the hocks on the
list are as dear—notably the Steinberg Cabinet Auslese at 180s.
a dozen—no mean price for a bottle of wine in days when, as
this Harvey's list shows, one could buy a case of "pale old cognac"
for 60s. or 72s. a dozen.

Those who know Harvey's reputation for Peninsular wines may be surprised at the poor showing that port makes on the list. True there is some 1847 in half-bottles, and "old bottled port" of unspecified age, but there is not the range one might expect. The fact is that at this time port was in low repute. T. C. Shaw, a wine-merchant and author, writing in 1864 said of port, "it cannot be denied that it is now generally regarded as an intoxicating vulgar wine". The cause of this was the very poor quality of much port then being shipped to England—and its subsequent "treatment" by irresponsible merchants, who coloured it and sweetened it—and did even worse.

Sherry, on the other hand, was in high esteem. Shaw reported that "for some years the demand for sherry has quite surpassed the supply". He then goes on to complain of the absence of old *soleras* to give quality to the blends which were shipped. Harvey and White offer no fewer than 17 sherries, ranging in price from 30*s*. to 72*s*. a dozen. They are also to be bought in butts of 108 gallons. Next to the list of the sherries appears an assortment of wines, once on every wine merchant's list, but now scarcely to be found in this country, including Lisbon, Bucellas Hock, Calcavella; these Peninsular wines were gradually driven out by the finer wines of France. The same applies to Voslauer, "Austrian claret", to be bought at 2*s*. a bottle.

Among the champagnes, names still to be found on Harvey's list today were listed, including Perrier Jouët, Moet et Chandon, Veuve Clicquot and Roederer. Sparkling moselle is offered in surprising variety.

A note at the bottom of the list suggests the long credit that wine merchants were then expected to give—"Six Months' Credit, or Five per Cent. Discount for prompt payment".

It is interesting to compare these prices of about ninety years ago with two other lists, the first issued as the Second World War began in the autumn of 1939, the second, the firm's latest list, dated 1955. In 1939 nearly all the wines were listed at dozen rates, but in 1955 these would often look a little terrifyingly high. Thus Bristol Cream was down at 156*s*. as against 28*s*. 6*d*. a bottle today. The 1939 list of sherries was formidable—thirty-six of them; opposite this was a list of twenty-four old bottled sherries, with bottling dates going back to 1919. Old bottled sherry is a connoisseur's delight, and is scarcely to be found now, although Harvey's hope to reintroduce them to their list shortly. As a rule it is the fuller sherries that benefit from age in bottle. Ports could be had sixteen years ago ranging back to the 1897 vintage; today they stop at 1922, which is about as old as is safe

to offer on any scale. One of the differences between pre-war
lists of wine merchants and those today is the shortage of old
wine, partly owing to the war, and partly to a run of indifferent
vintages in the 1930's. Before the war Harvey's could offer
clarets and burgundies twenty years old; today fine pre-war red
wine is hard to come by. As a result wines are being drunk when
they are much younger. In 1939 Harvey's were offering the 1934's
for laying down only. Nowadays, claret of five years old, and less,
is being drunk steadily.

And what wine could be bought in 1939! And at what prices!
Fine French wine was probably cheaper in the nineteen-thirties
than at any other time. From Harvey's one could buy the fine
Château Lafite 1929 for 8s. 6d. a bottle, the delicious Château
Latour 1924 for 11s. 4d.; fine but less aristocratic wines of the
great 1929 vintage could be bought château-bottled for as little
as 6s. On the other hand, Harvey's 1955 list has a much greater
range of clarets and burgundies—and indeed of German and
French white wines; let us hope that the red wines, which need
bottle-age, survive to reach maturity!

E. P.-R.

INDEX

The numerals in heavy type *denote the figure numbers of the illustrations*